Manual on the Wearing of Religious Symbols in Public Areas

D1666744

Council of Europe Manuals

HUMAN RIGHTS IN CULTURALLY DIVERSE SOCIETIES

Manual on the Wearing of Religious Symbols in Public Areas

by

Malcolm D. Evans

COUNCIL   CONSEIL
OF EUROPE   DE L'EUROPE

MARTINUS NIJHOFF PUBLISHERS

LEIDEN · BOSTON

2009

This book is printed on acid-free paper.

ISBN   Set   978 90 04 17274 6
       Manual on Religious Symbols   978 90 04 17276 0
       Manuel sur le discours de haine 978 90 04 17275 3

Koninklijke Brill NV incorporates the imprints Brill, Hotei Publishers, IDC Publishers, Martinus Nijhoff Publishers and VSP.

http://www.brill.nl

PRINTED IN THE NETHERLANDS.

ToC

Annexes

#1 General Introduction

The origins of this Manual lie in the increasing interest and importance of questions concerning the manner in which the freedom of religion and belief is to be enjoyed in Europe today. Issues concerning religion and belief have arisen in different ways at different times, reacting to the overall social and political context and the responses to this have differed greatly from one country to another. It is, then, not surprising that as social and political contexts evolve, new questions concerning the enjoyment of the freedom of thought, conscience and religion come to the fore and call for reflection and response. European history is closely intertwined with evolving patterns of religious and non-religious belief.[1] Indeed, the system of sovereign states which characterises the composition of modern Europe owes its origins to the struggle to separate political governance from religious governance and affiliations. Tragically, European history is punctuated by many instances of conflict between followers of various religious beliefs, and of persecution by both the religious and by the non-religious of those who either did not share or who rejected the belief systems of the dominant groups within the societies of which they formed a part.

There have been a variety of responses to instances of this nature over time. An early response was to seek to 'solve' the problem by working towards a situation in which each political community was religiously heterogeneous – an approach reflected in the Latin maxim 'cuius regio, eius religio', perhaps more easily understood as the proposition that the religious beliefs of the people should be the same as the religious beliefs of their rulers. In fact, such an approach negated the very idea of belief for most of the people, since

---

1   For an overview see Malcolm Evans, *Religious Liberty and International Law in Europe* (Cambridge: Cambridge University Press, 1997, reprinted 2008).

it meant that their beliefs depended on the beliefs of others: if their rulers were to change their beliefs, the people would have to change theirs as well. Naturally, for those who took their beliefs seriously this was an impossible state of affairs and inevitably gave rise to conflict. In order to reduce tensions, a further development came about with states recognising the legitimacy of a limited number of beliefs which they would allow to be practised within their territories. However, for as long as the governance of a state was premised upon the primacy of a particular pattern of religious belief, this always carried with it the risk of persecution should minority beliefs cease to be tolerated. Moreover, for as long as religious affiliation was seen as a marker of 'belonging' to the state itself, those who chose not to adhere to the dominant religious tradition(s) would inevitably be seen as presenting a potential threat to the political elites, and even when they presented no threat at all, were capable of being portrayed as posing a potential threat when it suited the interests of those in authority to do so, rendering them permanently vulnerable.

As long ago as the early seventeenth century, however, powerful voices called for a different approach. The influential international jurist, Alberico Gentili, writing shortly before the onset of the 30 Years War that tore apart central Europe and, through the Peace of Westphalia in 1648 gave birth to the modern system of European statehood, argued that:

> 'Religion is a matter of the mind and of the will, which is always accompanied by freedom.... Religion ought to be free. (I)f truly the profession of a different form of religious belief by their subjects does not harm princes, we are ... unjust... if we persecute those who profess another religion than our own.'[2]

This is a plea that still resonates today and which is yet to be fully realised. Ever since the triumph of the Enlightenment as reflected in the writings of Locke and in its realisation in the Revolutions of the late Eighteenth century, the idea that individuals should exercise the freedom of thought and of conscience in matters of religion and of belief has become increasingly well established and is now universally acknowledged. The more pressing difficulty became how this

---

2   Alberico Gentili, *De Iure Belli Libri Tres*, book I, Chapter IX.

might be realised in an age which recognised the right of states to regulate their own affairs free from pressure from others.

Once again, a variety of approaches were drawn upon. Some states continued the old tradition of entering into treaty relations which permitted them to exercise a degree of oversight and even intervention of the manner in which particular forms of believers were treated. Others insisted that the rights of believers continue to be respected when territory was transferred from sovereignty of one state to that of another. These practices came together in the mid to late nineteenth century when it became increasingly common to require newly constituted states to make commitments regarding their treatment of potentially vulnerable groups at the time of their recognition as members of the international community. But how to enforce such commitments without embroiling states in strife remained an unsolved challenge. The beginnings of a solution emerged after the First World War when many of the newly created or territorially reconfigured states in Central and Eastern Europe entered into a series of undertakings concerning minority populations – including commitments regarding their freedom of religion and beliefs – which were to be overseen and guaranteed not by other states but by the international community in the guise of the League of Nations. Tragically, these measures proved inadequate to prevent the horrors that culminated in the Second World War but they did lay the foundations for the emergence of the modern system of human rights protection which now provides the means and mechanisms for the protection of the rights not just of certain minorities in some countries within Europe, but of all those within the jurisdiction of member states of the Council of Europe. Moreover, whilst historically the focus has been very much on questions concerning religion and religious believers, the human rights framework adopts a different approach.

Human rights look to the person as a whole and at their place in the society of which they form a part. They do not seek to differentiate one person from another, or to value one group – or any one set of beliefs (religious or otherwise) – more than others. They seek to provide a means by which to reconcile the various conflicting interests which inevitably exist within any democratic state in which different understandings and different points of view co-exist

Human rights look to the person as a whole and at their place in the society of which they form a part. They do not seek to differentiate one person from another, or to value one group – or any one set of beliefs (…) – more than others.

side by side. They seek to protect the individual from overly intrusive state activities, whilst at the same time requiring that the state provides a balanced framework that permits everyone to enjoy their rights to the fullest extent that is compatible with the rights and freedoms of others. Whilst recognising that this is, first and foremost, a responsibility of the state itself, human rights are nevertheless a product of an international understanding of the basic rights and obligations of persons within a democratic political community and are properly subject to international scrutiny and, in contested cases, determination. The European Convention on Human Rights provides the premier means through which these aims are to be achieved within the community of European states as formed by the Council of Europe.

The need to find a means of accommodating religious diversity has played a significant role in the shaping of not only modern Europe but of the international legal system itself. In addition, the manner in which such accommodations have been achieved has varied over time, and has left its own historical legacy which still has reverberations today. Thus some still may hanker for the religiously homogenous state, in which a single belief system holds sway. Some may seek to manage religious life through the recognition of a limited number of authorised religions with whom they have a working relationship, denying legitimacy to those not officially approved. Others may seek to adopt an approach which insulates the apparatus of the state from matters of religion and belief, separating the spheres of the religious and spiritual from that of the political governance of society altogether. All of these – and other – approaches to the question have their roots in historical experiences and practices which reflected the dominant conceptual understandings of their times. Although these may still echo down the ages, the legitimacy of such approaches must today be assessed in the light of the requirements of the human rights framework to which they must either conform, or yield. This is the situation which is found in Europe today and forms the background to this Manual.

Different approaches to accommodating religious diversity have their roots in historical experiences. The legitimacy of such approaches must today be assessed in the light of the requirements of international human rights law.

The framework of the Convention in general, and the manner in which it relates to the freedom of thought, conscience and religion in particular, will be considered in detail in Section II of this Manual. Section III will identify the key concepts which have been identified in the jurisprudence of the Court and Sections IV and V will consider the role and responsibilities of the state and of individuals. These Sections are essential to properly understand the central issues which this Manual seeks to address – the wearing of religious symbols in public areas. Section VI will then look at a number of key definitional issues which need to be addressed. Section VII then sets out in summary fashion the essential questions which policy makers need to ask when addressing issues concerning the wearing of religious symbols. The final section of the Manual, Section VIII, seeks to apply these principles and approaches to a number of key areas and issues. For readers with limited time, Sections VII and VIII might be read separately. For the reader with very little time, Section VII (b) offers a succinct statement of the essential issues which need to be considered.

The Freedom of Thought, Conscience and Religion: An Introduction

Article 9 provides that

1. Everyone has the right to freedom of thought, conscience and religion: this right includes freedom to change his religion or belief and freedom, either alone or in community with others and in public or private, to manifest his religion or belief, in worship, teaching, practice or observance.
2. Freedom to manifest one's religion shall be subject only to such limitations as are prescribed by law and are necessary in a democratic society in the interests of public safety, for the protection of public order, health or morals, or for the protection of the rights and freedoms of others.

This is a classic human rights formulation, found in all the major human rights instruments, and sets out a very clear right which is to be enjoyed by the individual person, whilst subjecting it to a range of potential limitations intended to safeguard the interests of other individuals or a variety of community interests. This section looks at how Article 9 is constructed and operates in practice in order that a better understanding can be had of how it applies in the context of religious symbols,[1] which will be explored in detail in the later sections of this Manual.

---

1   There are now numerous monograph length works which examine Article 9 in some detail, including, Malcolm Evans, *Religious Liberty and International Law in Europe* (Cambridge: Cambridge University Press, 2007, reprinted 2008); Caroline Evans, *Freedom of Religion under the European Convention on Human Rights* (Oxford: Oxford University Press, 2001); Paul Taylor, *Freedom of Religion: UN and European Human Rights Law and Practice* (Cambridge: Cambridge University Press, 2005); Renata Uitz, *Europeans and their Rights: Freedom of Religion* (Strasbourg: Council of Europe Publishing, 2007). For a valuable work exploring the practice relating to a form of religious clothing see Dominic

(A) The *'Forum Internum'*

Article 9(1) opens by stating that 'everyone enjoys the freedom of thought, conscience and religion'. This provides an essential starting point, and the Convention bodies have frequently emphasised that 'Article 9 primarily protects the sphere of personal beliefs and religious creeds, i.e. the area which is sometimes called the *forum internum'*. It represents the sphere of 'inner conviction' and as such is absolutely inviolable. This makes it clear that individuals are free to adhere to any form of belief that they wish. The reason for this, as the Court acknowledged in the case of *Kosteski v. the former Yugoslav Republic of Macedonia*[2] is that 'the notion of the state sitting in judgment on the state of a citizen's inner and personal beliefs is abhorrent and may smack unhappily of past infamous persecutions'. Believing what one wishes does not, however, carry with it the right to act as one wishes and the second element of Article 9(1) moves beyond the *'forum internum'* to address the situation which arises when a person wishes to act in accordance with what they understand their pattern of thought, conscience or religion to mean for them. First, it expressly protects the right of a person to change their religion or belief – something which arises naturally from the first part of the Article allowing unfettered freedom of thought, conscience and religion. Secondly, it expressly recognises that individuals have the right to 'manifest' their religion or belief. However, the 'manifestation' of religion or belief is not unfettered and may be subject to limitations, provided such restrictions are in accordance with the provisions of Article 9(2).

> Personal beliefs and religious creeds represent the sphere of 'inner conviction' and as such are absolutely inviolable.

It is, then, essential to understand what falls within the scope of the *'forum internum'* and what falls beyond. This is a particularly important question when considering issues concerning religious symbols but since it can only be properly considered once the general scheme of Article 9 has been looked at, it will be returned to later. Apart from frequently re-iterating its view that the protection of the *forum internum* is the primary purpose of Article 9, the Court has said relatively little about it. As a result of this, it is only possible to discern its scope by examining what falls

---

McGoldrick, *Human Rights and Religion: The Islamic Headscarf Debate in Europe* (Oxford: Hart Publishing, 2006).

2   *Kosteski v. the former Yugoslav Republic of Macedonia*, no. 55170/00, para 39, 13 April 2006

within the ambit of the so called '*forum externum*', perhaps better described as the sphere of external manifestation, to which considerable attention has been paid.

(B) The Manifestation of Religion or Belief

Understanding what is meant by the 'manifestation' of religion or belief lies at the heart of the proper application of Article 9 and it presents a series of difficult questions, which will be considered in turn.

(a) What is a 'religion or belief' for the purposes of Article 9?

The protection of the '*forum internum*' extends to all patterns of 'thought, conscience and religion' whereas it is the manifestation of 'religion or belief' which is protected (and limited by) the second part of Article 9(1) and by Article 9(2). Does this mean that patterns of thought and conscience of a non-religious nature are not covered by the 'freedom to manifest'; that is, is the word 'belief' a synonym for 'religion', or does it also extend the freedom to manifest to all forms of thought and conscience? This question was considered by the European Commission on Human Rights in the case of *Arrowsmith v. the United Kingdom* in which the Commission was of the view that 'pacifism as a philosophy .... falls within the ambit of the right to freedom of thought and conscience. This attitude of pacifism may therefore be seen as a belief ("conviction") protected by Article 9(1)'.[3]

This broad, inclusive approach which places all forms of belief on an equal footing has been followed consistently ever since. Nevertheless, this does not mean that any form of belief will 'qualify' for the purposes of Article 9(1). First, there are some forms of belief which might be considered incompatible with Convention values altogether and so cannot benefit from its protection at all. For example, Article 17[4] of the Convention expressly seeks to prevent its

Understanding what is meant by the 'manifestation' of religion or belief lies at the heart of the proper application of Article 9 and it presents a series of difficult questions: i. What is a 'religion or belief' for the purposes of Article 9?; (ii) What is a manifestation?; (iii) When is an 'interference' attributable to the state?

---

3   *Arrowsmith v. UK*, no. 7050/77, Commission Report of 12 October 1978, Decisions and Reports 19, p. 5, para 69.

4   Article 17 provides: 'Nothing in this Convention may be interpreted as implying for any state, group or person any right to engage in any activity or perform any act aimed at the destruction of any

provisions being used to undermine essential convention
values. Although the Court has not used Article 17 to remove the protections offered by Article 9 to believers, this
remains possible in appropriate cases.[5] This will always be
exceptional, however, and the more common situation will
be one in which the nature of the belief in question, whilst
fully consonant with Convention values, is not of a nature
which attracts the direct protection of Article 9. For example, under Article 10 of the Convention the freedom of expression is extended to 'opinions' and 'ideas'. 'Manifestation'
is, however, a broader notion than 'expression' and so it is
necessary to consider what is needed to elevate an 'opinion'
or an 'idea' which might be expressed under Article 10 into
a 'belief' which may be manifested under Article 9.[6]

The Court has studiously avoided saying whether it considers particular forms of 'belief' to be religious in nature and
since it is not necessary for it to do so in order to be able to
apply Article 9 this is a wise approach. It is, however, clear
that it considers that what might reasonably be described as
the 'mainstream' religious traditions – such as Buddhism,
Christianity, Hinduism, Islam, Judaism, Sikhism – all fall
within its scope and it has acknowledged that it embraces
Jehovah's Witnesses, the Church of Scientology and many
others besides. Its applicability to cogent bodies of thought

---

of the rights and freedoms set forth herein or at their limitation to
a greater extent than is provided for in the Convention'.

5   For example, in *Norwood v. the United Kingdom*, the Court found
    that the display of a poster by a member of an extreme right wing
    party that identified Islam as a religion with terrorism amounted
    to a 'vehement attack on a religious group' was 'incompatible with
    the values proclaimed and guaranteed by the convention, notably
    tolerance, social peace and non-discrimination' and, as such,
    could not benefit from the protection of Article 10, the freedom of
    expression. *Norwood v. the United Kingdom* (dec.), no. 23131/03,
    ECHR 2004-XI.

6   In the *Arrowsmith* case the European Commission implicitly
    endorsed the view of the respondent UK Government that whilst
    'ideas' and 'opinions' were indeed protected under Article 10, the
    use of the term 'belief' in Article 9 indicated a somewhat higher
    threshold and this was confirmed by the Court in the case of
    Campbell and Cosans v. the United Kingdom where it said that 'the
    term 'belief' denotes views that attain a certain level of cogency,
    seriousness, cohesion and importance'. See *Campbell and Cosans
    v. the United Kingdom*, judgment of 25 February 1982, Series A no.
    48, para 36.

of a non-religious nature, such as atheism and pacifism, is also well attested. More difficulty has been occasioned by less well established patterns of thought, or by beliefs which, though sincerely held, do not offer up an overall 'guiding outlook' of a similarly encompassing nature.

The difficulties that may be faced are well illustrated by the case of *Pretty v. the United Kingdom*.[7] The applicant in this case suffered from a terminal illness and wished to die but needed assistance in order to commit suicide. Her husband was in principle willing to assist in this, but in practice was unwilling to do so as this would involve him committing what was a criminal offence under the domestic law. Mrs Pretty argued that this breached her rights under Article 9 since she 'believed in and supported the notion of assisted suicide'. The Court rejected this here, taking the view that 'not all opinions and convictions constitute beliefs in the sense protected by Article 9(1) of the Convention'. In order to determine whether the belief was of a nature which attracted that protection, the Court looked to see if an act of 'worship, teaching, practice or observance' was at issue, and concluded that it was not.[8] It chose to see the issue as being one of personal autonomy, properly protected under Article 8 of the Convention (concerning respect for family and private life). This suggests that largely personally-held ideas, opinion and beliefs, no matter how seriously taken, will not fall within the scope of Article 9 although they may qualify for protection under other provisions of the convention.[9] The critical point, however, is that they then do not benefit from the particular protections offered to the 'manifestation' of religion or belief by Article 9.

(b) What is a 'manifestation'?

Once it has been determined that a form of belief does indeed 'qualify' for the purposes of Article 9, the next question to be asked is whether the activities or behaviour which have been undertaken on the basis of that form of belief are to be considered as amounting to a form of mani-

---

7   *Pretty v. the United Kingdom*, no. 2346/02, ECHR 2002-III.

8   *Ibid*, para 81.

9   But see *Plattform "Arzte fur das Leben" v. Austria*, judgment of 21 June 1988, Series A no. 139, in which Article 9 was said to extend to the members of an association of doctors opposed to abortion.

festation. The Convention itself lists four particular forms of manifestation: worship, teaching, practice and observance. The Court has hinted on several occasions that this is not necessarily a definitive list and as will be seen later, it has interpreted Article 9 in a way which offers protection to interests which lie beyond this 'illustrative list'. Nevertheless, it will usually be necessary for applicants to be able to demonstrate that there has been an impediment placed upon their ability to engage in one of these activities in order to claim that their freedom to manifest their religion or belief has been infringed.

> The Convention lists four particular forms of manifestation: worship, teaching, practice and observance. It will usually be necessary for someone to be able to demonstrate that there has been an impediment placed upon his or her ability to engage in one of these activities.

One difficult issue concerns who is to decide whether a form of action is to be understood, in a *prima facie* sense, as a manifestation of a religion or belief at all. If the applicant asserts that something they have done was as a result of their religion or belief, is it open to the Court simply to deny that this is so on the basis of its scrutiny of the facts, or is it bound to accept the applicant's 'subjective' characterisation of their actions? This question arose in the case of *Valsamis v. Greece*, in which a child was excluded from school as a result of her parents' refusal to allow her to participate in a parade commemorating the national day of independence. The parents argued that the parade commemorated war (and was preceded by an official Mass and followed by military parades) and so was incompatible with the family's pacifist beliefs as members of the Jehovah's Witnesses. The Court (as had the Commission before it) rejected this contention, arguing that 'it can discern nothing, either in the purposes of the parade or in the arrangements for it, which could offend the applicants' pacifist convictions...'[10] and concluded that 'the obligation to take part in the school parade was not such as to offend her parents' religious convictions.'[11] This approach is problematic since it is difficult to see on what basis a Court can determine that a person does not understand an issue to be of a religious nature if they say that, for them, it is.

This does not mean that an applicant's characterisation of an act as a manifestation must be accepted in an unquestioning fashion. For example, if a person is seeking to take advantage of a privilege or exemption which is available

---

10   *Valsamis v. Greece*, judgment of 18 December 1996, *Reports of Judgments and Decisions* 1996-VI, para 31.

11   *Ibid*, para 37.

only to adherents of a particular religious tradition or belief system it may be necessary to consider whether that person genuinely is an adherent of the belief system in question.[12] However, particular care needs to be taken when adopting such an approach in the context of the wearing or religious symbols. Compelling a person to prove their religious allegiance might indeed become oppressive, and will almost certainly be oppressive if the 'the privileges' in question are intimately connected with the practice of one's belief. It could be argued that by wearing a religious symbol a person is not only acting in a fashion which they consider to be consonant with their belief system, but that that very act itself demonstrates their *bona fides* adherence to that belief and so no further exploration of the question is necessary. However, the need to determine whether a particular form of jewellery, clothing, etc is indeed being worn as a religious symbol or in a religious sense or whether it is being worn for other reasons, such as comfort, social conformity, fashion, – or even disrespect of religion – may indeed need to be explored in order to determine whether an issue arises under Article 9.

Even when it is clear that the activity in question is to be taken as a *bona fide* form of manifestation by the applicant, this does not necessarily mean that it is to be taken as a form of manifestation *for the purposes of Article 9*. For example, the *Arrowsmith* case concerned a pacifist who had been distributing leaflets outside an army camp which gave information on how soldiers might claim exemption from serving in a situation of conflict. As far as the applicant was concerned, she was engaged in the practice of pacifism

---

12   For example, in the case of *Kosteski v. the former Yugoslav Republic of Macedonia*, op.cit., the applicant argued that his '*forum internum*' had been violated by his being required to prove his status as a practising Muslim before he could take advantage of the right enjoyed by all Muslims in the former Yugoslav Republic of Macedonia to absent himself from work in order to attend a religious festival. The Court accepted that 'the notion of the state sitting in judgement on the state of a citizen's inner and personal beliefs is abhorrent'. However, it went on to say that 'it is not oppressive or in fundamental conflict with freedom of conscience to require some level of substantiation when the claim concerns a privilege or entitlement not commonly available' (para 39). This reflects the approach taken in cases concerning conscientious objection to military service, and it is obviously appropriate to confirm that those claiming to be manifesting a belief are doing so *bona fides*.

and as such her actions fell within the protective reach of Article 9. The Commission took the view that whilst the manifestation of pacifism was indeed protected by Article 9 the distribution of leaflets such as those at issue in the case in hand was not. It accepted that the applicant had been 'motivated by her pacifist beliefs' when she distributed them but it did not think that this amounted to a 'manifestation', observing that 'it is true that public declarations proclaiming generally the idea of pacifism and urging the acceptance of a commitment to non-violence may be considered as a normal and recognised manifestation of pacifist belief. However, when the actions of individuals do not actually express the belief concerned they cannot be considered to be as such protected by Article 9(1)'.[13] In consequence, and in a passage still regularly cited by the Court, the Commission concluded that 'the term "practice" as employed in Article 9(1) does not cover each act which is motivated or influenced by a religion or a belief'.[14] Thus not all activities undertaken which are motivated or inspired by a belief are necessarily protected since not only might they not be related to the '*forum internum*' and the sphere of 'inner conviction' but they may also be considered not to amount to a *manifestation* of that belief for the purposes of Article 9(1).

(c) When is an 'interference' attributable to the state?

An additional question is whether a person's inability to manifest their religion or belief is something for which the state is responsible, or whether it is largely attributable to choices which those individuals have freely made for themselves. For example, a number of cases have considered the question of whether employees may be required to work on days or at times which prevent them from fulfilling their religious obligations. In the case of *X v. the United Kingdom*[15] it was decided that there had been no interference with the freedom of religion or belief by requiring the applicant, a Muslim teacher, to work at a given time on a Friday afternoon when he believed he ought to be at prayer since he remained free to renegotiate his contract, or change his employment altogether. His inability to attend prayers was

---

13   *Arrowsmith v. UK*, op.cit., para 71.
14   *Ibid.*
15   *X. v. the United Kingdom*, no 8160/78, Commission decision of 12 March 1981, Decisions and Reports 22, p. 27, para 36.

a result of his choosing to accept a full time position as a teacher rather than as a result of a restriction placed upon him. A similar approach was taken in the case of *Konttinen v. Finland*,[16] where the applicant was a Seventh Day Adventist who objected to being required to work after sunset on a Friday on the grounds that this was forbidden by his religious beliefs, and also (*inter alia*) in *Stedman v. the United Kingdom*,[17] where the applicant's employer, following a change in national legislation, required the applicant to work on Sunday. In all these cases there was no doubt that the applicants were either unable to engage in acts of worship or to engage in a form of religious observance but the Court (or Commission) was of the view that this was attributable not to the actions of the state but to choices made voluntarily by the applicants. In short, the solution to their difficulties lay in their own hands. If they wished to prioritise their religious observance above their contractual commitments as employees, they could do so by changing the nature of their employment.

> The Court will examine whether a person's inability to manifest their religion or belief is something for which the state is responsible, or whether it is largely attributable to choices which those individuals have freely made for themselves.

Similar outcomes have been reached in different contexts. For example, in *Pichon and Sajous v. France*,[18] the applicants were pharmacists who objected on religious grounds from being required to sell contraceptives. The Court took the view that since they were free to take up a different profession there was no interference with their freedom to manifest their religion.[19] In the case of *Cha'are Shalom Ve Tsedek v. France*[20] the Court decided that there had been no interference with the right of the applicant association in prohibiting its members from engaging in ritual slaughter of animals in order to ensure that the meat produced was religiously acceptable since such meat could be acquired in and imported from Belgium. Finally, in *Kalaç v. Turkey,* in which a military judge was dismissed from his position on account of his membership of a religious community whose

---

16   *Konttinen v. Finland,* no. 24949/94, Commission decision of 3 December 1996, Decisions and Reports 87, p. 68.

17   *Stedman v. the United Kingdom,* no 29107/95, Commission decision of 9 April 1997, Decisions and Reports 87- A, p. 104.

18   *Pichon and Sajous v. France* (dec.), no 49853/99, ECHR 2001-X.

19   The Court might also have considered whether their desire not to sell contraceptives amounted to a manifestation at all, or whether it was a stance which was merely 'motivated' by their beliefs.

20   *Cha'are Shalom Ve Tsedek v. France* [GC], no. 27417/95, ECHR 2000-VII.

views were, in the view of the military authorities, inimical to the proper functioning of a judge, the Court concluded that 'His compulsory retirement was not an interference with his freedom of conscience, religion or belief but was intended to remove from the military legal service a person who had manifested his lack of loyalty to the foundation of the Turkish nation, namely secularism, which it was the task of the armed forces to guarantee.'[21]

Thus whilst the Convention protects the freedom to manifest one's religion or belief, applicants may be expected to take whatever steps are available to them to ensure that they can act in accordance with their beliefs – even if this is at some personal cost to them – before the Court will conclude that an interference attributable to the state has occurred. There are, however, limits to this approach. If the burdens placed on an applicant are particularly onerous, they might amount to a form of pressure which affects their very ability to adhere to the pattern of thought, conscience and religion of their choice. Such a degree of pressure could amount to a form of coercion which would be incompatible with the requirements of Article 9(1). Similarly, it may be that if the burdens placed on adherents of some beliefs are greater than those placed on others, and there is no objective justification for this difference, then questions of discrimination in the enjoyment of the right will come into play and may result in a violation of the Article. This will be considered in greater detail later, but the approach can be illustrated at this point by looking at the decision of the European Commission in the case of *Choudhury v. the United Kingdom*[22] in which an application concerning the failure of the blasphemy laws in the United Kingdom to extend protection to the Islamic faith was declared inadmissible. The Commission was of the view that the inability of the applicant to ensure that criminal proceedings were brought against the author and publisher of a book which, in his view, amounted to a 'scurrilous attack' on his religion did not give rise to a claim under Article 9 since there had been no interference with his ability of manifest his freedom of religion of belief. Moreover, it thought that no issue was raised in relation to Article 14 of the Convention

> Whilst the Convention protects the freedom to manifest one's religion or belief, applicants may be expected to take whatever steps are available to them to ensure that they can act in accordance with their beliefs.

---

21 *Kalaç v. Turkey*, judgment of 1 July 1997, *Reports of Judgments and Decisions* 1997-IV, paras 25 and 30.

22 *Choudhury v. the United Kingdom*, no. 17439/90, Commission decision of 5 March 1991, unreported.

(non discrimination in the enjoyment of a convention right) since nothing had occurred that fell within the scope of the rights recognised by Article 9. As will be seen below, the Court subsequently adopted a different approach to this latter point in the case of *Otto-Preminger Institut* v. *Austria*, in so far as it decided that the Article 9 rights might indeed be violated by 'provocative portrayals of objects of religious veneration' and that 'a state may legitimately consider it necessary to take measures aimed at repressing certain forms of conduct .... judged incompatible with the respect for the freedom of thought, conscience and religion of others'.[23] In light of this, it would seem that the failure of the state to offer the same degree of legal protection against the 'provocative portrayal of objects of religious veneration' to one form of religion or belief as it offers to another would now amount to a violation of the Convention. This too has important consequences as regards the wearing of religious symbols, and will be explored further below.

(C)   Restrictions upon the Manifestation of Religion or Belief

Although actions which amount to a manifestation of a religion are belief are protected under Article 9(1), they may be subject to limitations from two sources. First, Article 15 permits states to derogate from their obligations under a number of Convention Articles, including Article 9, 'in times of war or other public emergencies threatening the life of the nation' but only 'to the extent strictly required by the exigencies of the situation'. In theory, this could be taken to suggest that in such emergency situations the state might be able to act in a manner which even impinged upon the *'forum internum'* – for example, seeking to persuade or coerce individuals to abandon forms of thinking or of belief which were considered inimical to national security. However, given the primarily personal and private scope of the *forum internum*, it is difficult to see how such intrusions could ever be 'strictly required'.[24] Although Article 15 does

---

23   *Otto-Preminger Institut v. Austria*, judgment of 20 September 1994, Series A no. 295-A, para 47.

24   Moreover, Article 3 of the Convention prohibits 'inhuman or degrading treatment' in absolute terms and is not subject to the limitations of Article 15 and it is difficult to see how activities capable of coercing a change in private patterns of thought would not fall foul of this provision.

provide a possible means of restricting the 'manifestation' of religion or belief to a degree beyond that permitted by Article 9(2) no state has yet considered there to be a need of such a nature in the few emergency situations which have given rise to notices of derogation and so it is unnecessary to do more than note that this is a theoretical possibility.

> Article 9(2) is the most significant source of possible restrictions on freedom to manifest one's religion or beliefs. Limitations must be 'prescribed by law', follow a 'legitimate aim' and be 'necessary in a democratic society'.

The second and most significant source of limitation is Article 9(2). In common with similar clauses in the Convention, it requires that limitations be both 'prescribed by law' and 'necessary in a democratic society', but with the state enjoying a certain margin of appreciation, each of which will be briefly considered.

(a) 'Prescribed by law'

The essence of the 'prescribed by law' requirement is captured in two ideas: first, that 'the law must be adequately accessible; the citizen must be able to have an indication that is adequate in the circumstances' and secondly, that the law must be 'formulated with sufficient precision to enable the citizen to regulate his conduct: he must be able to foresee to a degree that is reasonable in the circumstances, the consequences which a given action may entail'.[25] Both of these criteria call for a reasonableness-based assessment which can only be determined on the facts of each case, although the Court in *Hasan and Chaush v. Bulgaria* made it clear that, in combination, this means that in matters concerning fundamental rights 'it would be contrary to the rule of law ... for a legal discretion granted to the executive to be expressed in terms of an unfettered power'.[26]

Hasan and Chaush was one of the first cases concerning Article 9 in which it was decided that a restriction had not been 'prescribed by law'. The provisions at issue permitted the authorities to replace the chosen leader of the Muslim community in Bulgaria with a leader of their choice. The Court noted that 'the relevant law does not provide for any substantive criteria on the basis of which [the authorities] register denominations and changes of their leadership'

---

25   Sunday Times v. the United Kingdom (no. 1), judgment of 26 April 1979, Series A no. 30, para 49.

26   *Hasan and Chaush v. Bulgaria* [GC], no. 30985/96, para 84, ECHR 2000-XI.

and that there were 'no procedural safeguards ... against arbitrary exercise of the discretion left to the executive'.[27] A further illustration of this approach is provided by *Kuznetsov v. Russia*, in which the Chair of a regional Human Rights Commission broke up a meeting of a group of Jehovah's Witnesses in a fashion which was attributable to the state (in that she had purported to be acting in her official capacity, and was accompanied by uniformed police officers). The Court noted that 'the legal basis for breaking up a religious event conducted on the premises lawfully rented for that purpose was conspicuously lacking' and so had not been 'prescribed by law'.[28]

(b) *'Necessary in a democratic society'*

Once it has been determined that a restriction has been 'prescribed by law' for the purposes of Article 9(2), it is then necessary to determine whether it is 'necessary in a democratic society'. The Court has often stressed that 'the freedom of thought, conscience and religion is one of the foundations of a 'democratic society' and the necessity of any restriction will depend upon whether it fulfils a number of requirements.

The first is that the restriction pursues a legitimate aim as set out in article 9(2), these being public safety, the protection of public order, health or morals and the protection of the rights and freedoms of others. Though important, this is not a difficult hurdle to surmount.[29]

The second, and arguably more critical question, is whether the nature of the interference is proportionate to the legitimate aim which is being pursued, since it is this which will determine whether the interference could be considered as 'necessary'. The European Commission said that 'the "neces-

---

27 *Ibid*, para 85.

28 *Kuznetsov v. Russia*, no. 184/02, para 74, 11 January 2007.

29 For example, in *Casimiro v. Luxembourg* (dec.), no. 44888/98, 27 April 1999, the Court decided in a case brought by his parents that requiring a child who was a Seventh Day Adventist to attend state schooling on a Saturday, their religious day of rest, could be justified on the basis that it was aimed at securing the rights and freedoms of others; in that case, their own child's right to education.

sity test" cannot be applied in absolute terms but requires the assessment of various factors. Such factors include the nature of the right involved, the degree of interference, i.e. whether it was proportionate to the legitimate aim pursued, the nature of the public interest and the degree to which it requires protection in the circumstances of the case'.[30] This, then, sets up a complex factual matrix which has to be applied by the Court when assessing the necessity of an interference.

(c)   The margin of appreciation

It is at this point that the doctrine of the 'margin of appreciation' comes into play. The rationale for the 'margin of appreciation' was set out in the case of *Handyside v. the United Kingdom* in the following terms:[31]

> 'By reason of their direct and continuous contact with the vital forces or their countries, state authorities are in principle in a better position than the international judge to give an opinion on the exact content of these requirements as well as on the 'necessity' of a 'restriction' or 'penalty' intended to meet them.'

However, the Court has made it clear that the 'margin of appreciation' goes hand in hand with European oversight and that the breadth of the margin of appreciation accorded to states will vary depending on the rights and interests at stake, and that is very much a question for the Court itself to decide. In some areas, the Court has decided that very little, if any margin of appreciation is given to states. This is particularly true as regards matters in which it considers there to be a 'pan-European' consensus. However, there is no such consensus as regards Article 9. In the case of *Otto-Preminger Institut v. Austria* the Court said that 'it is not possible to discern throughout Europe a uniform conception of the significance of religion in society: even within a single country such conceptions may vary'.[32] The Court sees this as an area in which there is considerable variation

---

30   See *X and the Church of Scientology v. Sweden*, no 7805/77, Commission decision of 5 May 1979, Decisions and Reports 16, p. 68.

31   *Handyside v. the United Kingdom*, judgment of 7 December 1976, Series A no. 24, para 48.

32   *Otto-Preminger Institut v. Austria*, op.cit., para 56.

in practice and, in consequence, it grants states a relatively broad margin of appreciation. Thus in the case of *Leyla Şahin v. Turkey* – concerning the wearing of headscarves by students in universities in Turkey – the Court said 'Where questions concerning the relationship between state and religions are at stake, on which opinion in a democratic society may reasonably differ widely, the role of the national decision making body must be given special importance ... Rules in this sphere will consequently vary from one country to another according to national traditions .... Accordingly the choice of the extent and form such regulations should take must inevitably be left up to a point to the state concerned, as it will depend on the domestic context'.[33]

It cannot be overemphasised, however, that this does not give the state an unfettered discretion to determine whether a restriction is proportionate to the aim pursued. It has been persuasively argued that the margin of appreciation is a second order principle and that the state is constrained by an overarching primary principle of ensuring that there is a 'priority to rights'[34] and the Court itself has stressed that although the state enjoys considerable leeway – it does so only 'up to a point'. Not only is the national assessment subject to European scrutiny in order to ensure that it does indeed meet the requirements of proportionality on the facts of the case, but it is always open to the Court to narrow that margin should a more general consensus on the relationship between the state and the manifestation of religion or belief emerge. In the meanwhile, it also follows from this that different responses to similar situations will be acceptable within the Convention framework, providing that they properly reflect a balancing up on the particular issues in the contexts in which they emerge. This means that the decisions of the Court in relation to Article 9(2) must be treated with extreme caution: for example, just because a restriction on the wearing of a religious symbol has been upheld in one case does not mean that a similar restriction will be upheld in another, where the context may be very different.

> Where questions concerning the relationship between state and religions are at stake, on which opinion in a democratic society may reasonably differ widely, the role of the national decision-making body must be given special importance. However, this does not give the state an unfettered discretion to determine whether a restriction is proportionate to the aim pursued.

---

33   *Leyla Şahin v. Turkey* [GC], no. 44774/98, para 109, ECHR 2005-XI.

34   See S Greer, *The European Convention on Human Rights: Achievements, Problems and Prospects* (Cambridge University Press, 2006), pp. 201-213.

(D) The Education of Children

The place of religion in the educational system raises many difficult and delicate questions.

Children, as autonomous individuals, enjoy the freedom of religion or belief in their own right, as do adults. However, given the special interests of parents and legal guardians regarding the religious and philosophical upbringing of their children, the rights of the child in the sphere of education are often exercised by parents in their own right rather than in the name of the child. Thus Article 2 of the First Protocol to the European Convention provides that:

> 'No person shall be denied the right to education. In the exercise of any functions which it assumes in relation to education and to teaching, the state shall respect the right of parents to ensure such education and teaching in conformity with their own religious and philosophical convictions.'

Of course, there will come an age at which children may seek to assert their own rights in this regard, and one can expect that the rights enjoyed by the parents regarding the education of their children in accordance with their religious or philosophical convictions will transfer to the children themselves in a fashion commensurate with their evolving capacities.

As the child matures, the nature of the claim changes from the perspective of the freedom of religion or belief, since children do not have any greater rights than anyone else to be shielded from teaching not in accordance with their own religious or philosophical convictions. Therefore, their claims must be assessed in accordance with the more general approach of ensuring that the state, through its teachers, does not take undue advantage of the position that it enjoys *vis-à-vis* pupils to influence their views in an inappropriate fashion.

A number of definitional questions need to be briefly considered. Article 2 of the Protocol refers to parental, 'religious or philosophical convictions' whereas Article 9 of the Convention refers to 'religion or belief'. The meaning of this was explored in the case of *Campbell and Cosans v. the United Kingdom.* As has already been seen, the Court took the view that the word 'convictions' was to be equated with

'belief', both requiring 'a certain level of cogency, seriousness, cohesion and importance', thus differentiating them
from mere 'ideas' or 'opinions'.[35] However, it is only such
convictions (or beliefs) which are religious or philosophical in nature which attract the protection of the Article.
The Court has never defined the word 'religion', but it has
fleshed out its understanding of what is meant by 'philosophy'. In *Campbell and Cosans* the Court accepted that 'the
word "philosophy" bears numerous meanings: it is used to
allude to a fully fledged system of thought or, rather loosely,
to views on more or less trivial matters'. However, it thought
that 'neither of these two extremes can be adopted for
the purposes of interpreting Article 2' and concluded that
'"Philosophical Convictions" in the present context denotes
... such convictions as are worthy of respect in a "democratic society" and are not incompatible with human dignity'.[36]
Thus the Court adopts a rather subjective approach to this
important question.

A second point concerns what is meant by 'respect' for
parental convictions. The Court has said that 'The verb
"respect" means more than "acknowledge" or "take into
account" ... in addition to a primarily negative undertaking,
it implies some positive obligation on the part of the state'.[37]
Article 2 does *not* mean that a state is bound to provide a
system of education that accords with parental beliefs, but
it *does* mean that parents can object to the nature and content of the education and teaching given to their children
where religious instruction is predicated upon, intended
to or has the effect of projecting the truth (or falsity) of a
particular set of beliefs.

Whilst states have considerable latitude with respect
to providing religious instruction, they may not seek to
encourage pupils in a particular worldview through the
educational system against the wishes of the pupils' parents.
In consequence, parents must have the right to withdraw
their children from such forms of teaching. As the Court
reiterated in *Folgerø v. Norway*, 'the state, in fulfilling the
functions assumed by it in regards to education and teaching, must take care that information or knowledge included

35   *Campbell and Cosans v. the United Kingdom*, op.cit., para 36.
36   *Idem.*
37   *Idem.* See also *Folgerø and Others v. Norway* [GC], no. 15472/02,
      para 84 (c), ECHR 2007.

in the curriculum is conveyed in an objective, critical and pluralistic manner. The state is forbidden to pursue an aim of indoctrination that might be considered as not respecting parents' religious and philosophical convictions. That is the limit that must not be exceeded'.[38]

> The state is required to respect parental convictions, whether religious or philosophical, throughout the entire education programme.

It must also be stressed that Article 2 is not only of relevance to the teaching *of* religion or philosophical convictions in schools: it also applies to teaching *about* religions and philosophies in schools. Moreover, as the Court emphasised in the case of *Kjeldsen, Busk Madsen and Pederson* v. *Denmark*,[39] no distinction is to be drawn between religious instruction and other subjects: the state is required to respect parental convictions, whether religious or philosophical, throughout the entire education programme. Indeed, illustrative examples of decisions already drawn on in this Manual show that the scope of this right extends beyond the educational curricula itself and concerns matters of educational organisation – such as teaching on holy days[40] and participation in school parades.[41] It also goes further to include the ethos of the educational establishment itself and this raises important issues regarding religious symbols which will be explored later.

---

38 *Folgerø and Others v. Norway* [GC], ibid., para 84 (h).

39 *Kjeldsen, Busk Madsen and Pederson v. Denmark*, judgment of 7 December 1976, Series A no. 23, para 53.

40 *Casimiro v. Luxembourg* (dec.), op.cit.

41 *Valsamis v. Greece*, op.cit.

#III The Key Concepts Emerging from the Practice of the European Court of Human Rights

The previous Section set out the structural elements of Article 9 of the Convention and Article 2 of the First Protocol in a fairly schematic fashion with the intention of introducing the 'basic building blocks' of the legal framework relevant for and preparatory to a detailed consideration of human rights approaches to the wearing of religious symbols. It also sought to illustrate how the Court has interpreted these elements. Important though this is, it is even more important to understand how this framework applies in practice. Once it has been decided that there has been an interference with a *bona fide* manifestation of religion or belief, the essential question becomes whether that interference is justified in accordance with Article 9(2). This, ultimately, calls for a balancing of the rights and interests at stake and although the state enjoys a generous margin of appreciation in this regard, it is not unfettered. Whilst there may be no common European conception of the role of religion and belief in public life to inform the outcome, a number of key concepts have emerged which, reflecting core Convention values, provide clear benchmarks against which to assess the legitimacy of any restriction. Moreover, approaching Article 9 from this conceptually oriented fashion has had the additional effect of broadening its scope to embrace fact situations which might not otherwise easily 'fit' within the rather rigid, structural approach outlined above. In consequence, these concepts might be said to represent the 'spirit' rather than the 'letter' of Article 9 and they have proven to be particularly significant to issues regarding religious symbols.

Moreover, the Court has indicated in the case of *Kokkinakis v. Greece* that whilst there may not be a common European approach sufficient to narrow the breadth of the margin of appreciation, there is a general underlying principle drawn from general convention values which must be adhered to, this being that:

> Whilst there may be no common European conception of the role of religion and belief in public life to inform the outcome, a number of key concepts have emerged: (a) the principle of respect; (b) that of individual and community responsibility; and (c) non-discrimination in the enjoyment of rights.

'As enshrined in Article 9, freedom of thought, conscience and religion is one of the foundations of a "democratic society" within the meaning of the Convention. It is, in its religious dimension, one of the most vital elements that go to make up the identity of believers and their conception of life, but it is also a precious asset for atheists, agnostics, sceptics and the unconcerned. The pluralism indissociable from a democratic society, which has been dearly won over the centuries, depends on it.'[42]

This key statement is routinely reproduced in almost all cases concerning Article 9 and provides the essential background to the principles identified in this section, and which both flow from and further refine its implications. In this statement, the Court acknowledges the significance of the freedom of thought, conscience and religion to the individual and the role it plays in their sense of personal identity; it also recognises how important it is to ensure that there is space for this to be recognised if there is to be a flourishing of a democratic society. At the same time, it underlines the need to ensure that a democratic society is open and inclusive by highlighting the importance of pluralism. Rather than calling for a balancing between the public and the private, it calls for a balancing of interests within the 'public' sphere that reflects both the importance of rights enshrined in Article 9 to both the individual and to democratic society, with the implication that when these interests appear to conflict, a resolution is to be sought which seeks to maximise both, to the extent that this is possible.

(A)   the Principle of Respect

Perhaps the most important of all the principles to have emerged from the Convention case-law has been the principle of respect. 'Respect' for parental wishes in matters concerning the education of their children is expressly referred to in Article 2 of the First Protocol but it is not directly referred to in Article 9 of the Convention. Its centrality to the practical operation of the Convention framework was, however, made clear in the very first case which was decided by the Court on the basis of Article 9, this being *Kokkinakis v. Greece*. This case concerned a member of the

---

42   Kokkinakis v. Greece, judgment of 25 May 1993, Series A no. 260-A, para 31.

Jehovah's Witnesses who had been convicted for unlawful proselytism, a criminal offence under Greek law. At the heart of the case lay the question of balancing the right of the applicant to practice his religion by seeking to share his faith with others against the right of the state to intervene to protect others from unwanted exposure to his point of view. Although on the facts of the case it was decided that the interference had not been shown to be justified, the Court argued that it may be 'necessary to place restrictions on this freedom in order to reconcile the interests of the various groups and to ensure that everyone's beliefs are respected'.[43] The key, then, is to ensure that when exercising its responsibilities the state adopts an approach which reflects the degree of respect which is to be accorded to the beliefs in question, which may of course be religious or non religious in nature.

This approach was confirmed in the subsequent case of *Larissis and others v. Greece*, in which the applicants who were members of a Pentecostal church and were officers in the Greek Air Force were convicted of various offences connected with their attempts to convert both a number of junior airmen and a number of civilians (in their free time) to their beliefs. The Court noted that whilst the authorities were 'justified in taking some measures to protect the lower ranking airmen from improper pressure'[44] the applicants' conviction for seeking to convert the civilians could not be justified on the basis of Article 9(2) since 'the civilians whom the applicants attempted to convert were not subject to the pressure and constraints of the same kind as the airmen.[45] Both the *Kokkinakis* and the *Larissis* cases show that in a democratic society it is necessary to ensure that believers are able to manifest their beliefs by bringing them to the attention of others, and by trying to persuade others to their point of view or else the exchange of ideas which underpins a vibrant and plural democracy would be undermined. At the same time, both cases show that the state pursues a legitimate aim when it seeks to limit proselytising activities which run the risk of subjecting individuals to pressure which they might find it difficult to resist. As the Court said when distinguishing between the situation of the

---

43   *Ibid*, para 33.

44   *Larissis and others v. Greece*, judgment of 24 February 1998, *Reports of Judgments and Decisions*, 1998-I, para 54.

45   *Ibid*, para 59.

airmen from that of the civilians in the *Larissis* case, 'it is of
decisive significance that the civilians whom the applicants
attempted to convert were not subject to pressure and constraints of the same kind as the airmen'.[46]

This might be loosely characterised as meaning that the
role of the state in such situations is to ensure that there
is a 'level playing field' between all concerned; the one
side free to present their points of view, the other to reject
them. More precisely, it might be said that in order to
justify a restriction being placed upon a person who seeks
to present their views to another what is needed is a nexus
or relationship that places one party in a position in which
they are unable, or feel unable, to exercise an appropriate
degree of thought or reflection before adopting or express-
ing adherence to the belief placed before them; or that
their decision to adopt or express such adherence flows not
from an assessment or response to the belief itself but from
a perception that it would be prudent to agree, or to be
seen to be agreeing, with the person who presented those
beliefs to them. The underlying principle is that of ensuring
respect for the beliefs of others, given effect in this instance
by ensuring that those who enjoy 'superiority' over others,
educationally, socially, politically or in any other fashion,
are not unduly advantaged in an exchange of ideas.

The idea of 'respect' is even more evident in those cases
which have concerned the behaviour of non-believers
which has caused offence to believers. The leading case remains that of *Otto-Preminger-Institut* v. *Austria* which concerned the seizure and forfeiture of a film considered to be
blasphemous under Austrian law. In a case brought under
Article 10 (freedom the expression) the Commission had
considered the film to be predominantly satirical in nature
and felt its prohibition 'excludes any chance to discuss the
message of the film'. The Court, however, saw matters differently. It thought that the state has a 'responsibility to ensure
the peaceful enjoyment of the right guaranteed under
Article 9 to the holders of those beliefs and doctrines' but at
the same time it noted that 'Those who choose to exercise
the freedom to manifest their religion.... cannot reasonably
expect to be exempt from all criticism. They must tolerate and accept the denial by others of their religious beliefs
and even the propagation by others of doctrines hostile to

---

46   *Idem.*

their faith'.[47] This must indeed be true, or else the rights of believers to manifest and propagate their beliefs, as set out in the *Kokkinakis* and *Larissis* cases would be undermined. Indeed, quoting the *Handyside* case, the Court recalled that the freedom of expression embraced ideas which 'shock, offend or disturb the state or any sector of the population', this being one of the demands of maintaining a plural, tolerant and broadminded society.[48] However, the Court, quoting *Kokkinakis*, also observed that 'a state may legitimately consider it necessary to take measures aimed at repressing certain forms of conduct, including the imparting of information and ideas, judgement incompatible with the respect for the freedom of thought, conscience and religions of others' and in a passage now regularly found in its jurisprudence, the Court then went on to say that:

> 'The respect for the religious feelings of believers as guaranteed by Article 9 can legitimately be thought to have been violated by provocative portrayals of objects of religious veneration: and such portrayals can be regarded as malicious violation of the spirit of tolerance, which must also be a feature of democratic society.'[49]

Indeed, in the case of *Wingrove v. the United Kingdom*, which also concerned a refusal to authorise the release of an allegedly blasphemous film, the Court not only reiterated this but spoke of 'a *duty* to avoid as far as possible an expression that is, in regard to objects of veneration, gratuitously offensive to others and profanatory',[50] a view which it confirmed in the later case of *Murphy v. Ireland*.[51]

The idea that the state is under a duty to ensure that the deeply held views of believers (both religious and non-religious) are both tolerated and respected has the practical effect of expanding the scope of Article 9 quite considerably. If one were to limit oneself to the rather 'mechanical'

Believers and non-believers are entitled to the respect of those who hold to other forms of belief - even though, of course, there may be profound disagreement regarding the content of those views.

---

47   *Otto-Preminger-Institut v. Austria*, op.cit., para 47.
48   *Ibid*, para 49, quoting *Handyside v. the United Kingdom*, op.cit., para 49.
49   *Otto-Preminger Institut v. Austria*, op.cit., para 47.
50   *Wingrove v. the United Kingdom*, judgement of 25 November 1995, *Reports of Judgments and Decisions* 1996-V, para 52 (emphasis added).
51   *Murphy v. Ireland*, no. 44179/98, para 65, ECHR 2003-XI (extracts).

approach to Article 9 which was outlined in Section II of this Manual (but which still forms the basis of its interpretation and application) it might be argued that since even the most virulent comments or the most offensive portrayals of the beliefs of others do not prevent them from continuing to hold to their beliefs and to manifest them in worship, teaching, practice and observance, there had been no interference with their rights at all. However, the Court has wisely understood that it is difficult to maintain to one's beliefs and practices in a hostile environment since, as was said in the Chamber's judgment in the case of *Refah Partisi v. Turkey*, 'where the offending conduct reaches a high level of insult and comes close to a negation of the freedom of religion of others it loses the right to society's tolerance.'[52]

In conclusion, the we can see that through these cases the Court has developed the principle of 'respect' as a key factor when balancing the respective interests which are engaged by Article 9. Accordingly, believers and non-believers are entitled to the respect of those who hold to other forms of belief – even though, of course, there may be profound disagreement regarding the *content* of those views since respect for the believer does not necessarily entail respect for what is believed. This principle is to be taken into account when the necessity of any interference with the manifestation of a religion or belief is being assessed. There is, however, a reciprocal obligation on believers to show respect for the beliefs (religious or non religious) of others in what they do and say. Finally, it should be noted that whilst the principle of respect guides the assessment of the Court in weighing up the proportionality of an interference with the enjoyment of the right, the adoption of what the Court has itself described as a 'rather open-ended notion'[53] has the practical effect of reinforcing the need for European supervision of the margin of appreciation that is accorded to states.

(B) The Principle of Individual and Community Autonomy

Although less well developed than the principle of respect, the Convention also acknowledges a principle of autonomy,

---

52 *Refah Partisi (the Welfare Party) and* Others v. *Turkey*, nos. 41340/98, 41342/98, 41343/98 and 41344/98, para 75, 31 July 2001.

53 *Murphy v. Ireland*, op.cit., para 68.

which itself must be understood in the light of the dual nature of Article 9 as both an individual and as a community
right. In its early practice, the Commission suggested that
the freedom of thought, conscience and religion could only
be enjoyed in an individual capacity and only by a human
person but this position has been abandoned over time. The
first step was in the case of *X and the Church of Scientology v. Sweden* which confirmed that religious organisations
could bring claims on behalf of their members, bundling up
(so to speak) their members' individual claims.[54] This was
then further developed so that it is now fully accepted that
legal entities are themselves entitled to the protection of
Article 9 in their own right, as is shown by the plethora of
cases brought by religious organisations challenging state
decision-making concerning their legal status. Thus in the
case of the *Metropolitan Church of Bessarabia and Others v.
Moldova*, in which the applicant was challenging the refusal
of the state to register them as a religious entity under the
relevant domestic law, the Court said[55]

> '...since religious communities traditionally exist in the form
> of organised structures, Article 9 must be interpreted in
> the light of Article 11 of the Convention, which safeguards
> associative life against unjustified state interference. Seen
> in that perspective, the right of believers to freedom of
> religion, which includes the right to manifest one's religion
> in community with others, encompasses the expectation that
> believers will be allowed to associate freely, without arbitrary
> state intervention.'

It underlined this by going on to emphasise that 'the autonomous existence of religious communities is indispensable
for pluralism in a democratic society and is thus an issue at
the very heart of the protection which Article 9 affords'.[56]
The Court has adopted the same approach in cases brought
under Article 11, in which the applicant bodies claim that
it is their freedom of association which has been breached,
rather than their freedom of religion. The close synergy between these Articles is now well established, and in the case
of the *Moscow Branch of the Salvation Army v. Russia*, the
Court, after quoting the above passage from the Metropoli-

---

54   *X and the Church of Scientology v. Sweden*, op.cit.

55   *Metropolitan Church of Bessarabia and Others v. Moldova*, no.
      45701/99, para 118, ECHR 2001-XII.

56   *Idem.*

tan Church case, confirmed that 'While in the contest of Article 11 the Court has often referred to the essential role played by political parties in ensuring pluralism and democracy, associations formed for other purposes, including those proclaiming or teaching religion, are also important to the proper functioning of democracy'.[57]

As associations with legal personality, religious and non-religious organisations within the scope of Article 9 not only enjoy the protection of Article 11 (freedom of association) but also enjoy all other convention rights applicable to legal entities, such as the right of access to a court in *Canea Catholic Church v. Greece*[58] and the freedom of expression in *Murphy v. Ireland*.[59]

Just as individuals are entitled to have their sphere of inner beliefs – their *'forum internum'* – respected absolutely, so likewise is there a degree of enhanced protection for what might be called the *'forum internum'* of the associative life of an organisation. Thus the state is not to intrude into what are properly considered to be essentially internal issues. Just as it is not for the state to pass judgement on the beliefs of an individual, the state is not to take a view on the beliefs of the community: the Court has frequently said that 'the right to freedom of religion ... excludes any discretion on the part of the state to determine whether religious beliefs or the means used to express such beliefs are legitimate' .

> The right to freedom of religion excludes any discretion on the part of the state to determine whether religious beliefs or the means used to express such beliefs are legitimate'. Likewise, the state is not to intrude into matters of internal governance of faith communities.

Likewise, the state is not to intrude into matters of internal governance. For example, in a number of cases the Court has made it clear that the state should not seek to influence internal decision-making concerning matters of leadership. In the case of *Hasan and Chaush* v. *Bulgaria* the applicants claimed that the state had wrongfully involved itself in a dispute between two rivals for the leadership of the Muslim Community in Bulgaria by refusing to register a breakaway group, thus lending its support to the claim of another to the leadership of the whole community. As the Court said, 'Their effect was to favour one faction of the Muslim community... The acts of the authorities operated... to deprive

---

57 *Moscow Branch of the Salvation Army v. Russia*, no. 72881/01, para 61, ECHR 2006-XI.

58 *Canea Catholic Church v. Greece*, judgment of 16 December 1997, *Reports of Judgments and Decisions* 1997-VIII, para 41.

59 *Murphy v. Ireland*, op.cit., para 61.

the excluded leadership of any possibility of continuing to represent at least part of the Muslim community and of managing its affairs according to the will of that part of the community. There was therefore an interference with the internal organisation of the Muslim religious community and with the applicant's right to freedom of religion as protected by Article 9 of the Convention.'[60] In the subsequent case of the *Supreme Holy Council of the Muslim Community v. Bulgaria* the Court again stressed that 'state measures favouring a particular leader or group in a divided religious community.... would constitute an infringement of the freedom of religion.'[61]

Similarly, the state is not to intervene in other situations of doctrinal or internal dispute within a belief community and in those instances in which an applicant believes that the church or organisation is itself acting in a fashion which has infringed their freedom of religion or belief, the Court has stressed that all that is needed is to ensure that the person is free to leave should they wish to do so – as in the case of *Knudsen v. Norway*[62] where a minister of the state church objected to his being dismissed for refusing to carry out certain functions required of him because of his opposition to the Norwegian abortion laws. However, this does not mean that the communal life of the organisation is beyond scrutiny. Just as the state is entitled to satisfy itself that individuals genuinely hold the beliefs which they claim, so may the state seek to satisfy itself that the patterns of belief which a religious organisation claims to espouse are those which it actually espouses: the Court has acknowledged 'that "an associations" programme may in certain cases conceal objectives and intentions different from the ones it proclaims. To verify that it does not, the content of the programme must be compared with the actions of the association's leaders and the positions they embrace.'[63] It follows from this that it is open to the Court to determine whether those beliefs qualify for the protection of Article 9 (or Article 11), in both cases the decision ultimately turning on whether those beliefs are consonant with the principles

---

60   *Hasan and Chaush v. Bulgaria* [GC], op.cit., para 82.

61   *Supreme Holy Council of the Muslim Community v. Bulgaria*, no 39023/97, para 77, 16 December 2004.

62   *Knudsen v. Norway*, no 11045/84, Commission decision of 8 March 1985, Decisions and Reports 41, p. 247.

63   *Moscow Branch of the Salvation Army v. Russia*, op.cit., para 93.

of democratic governance which the Court has clearly identified as underpinning the Convention system.

The relevance of this dual dimension for the wearing of religious symbols flows from the fact that Article 9 expressly acknowledges that the individual's right of freedom of religion and belief is to be enjoyed 'in community with others' and both 'in public and in private'. As the case-law of the Court shows, the community element of the right goes beyond the mere coming together of individuals in the collective enjoyment of their individual freedom and extends to the recognition of an associative life which is to be protected as a necessary expression of that freedom. Within that religious associative life, individuals will be bound by its rules and the primary protection for their right to freedom of thought, conscience and religion lies in their being able to leave and disassociate themselves from the community. The state is to avoid entering into religious or doctrinal questions within that associative life, other than to test them for compatibility with the foundational convention values of democratic governance, pluralism and tolerance. It is not for the Court to comment on the practices of the religious community, although they may of course be limited in accordance with Article 9(2).

In the case of *the Moscow Branch of the Salvation Army* v. *Russia* the Court made it clear that the need to respect the internal affairs of a religious organisation extended not only to its organisational structures but also to the clothing worn by its members. It said that 'It is undisputable that for the members of the applicant branch, using ranks similar to those used in the military and wearing uniforms were particular ways of organising the internal life of their religious community and manifesting the Salvation Army's religious beliefs'.[64]

In this way, the internal and external and the individual and the community combine to permit a religious organisation to adopt particular forms of religious symbols and clothing, and for its members to manifest their beliefs by wearing them in the public space as well as in the private. Though always subject to proportionate restriction on legitimate grounds, the case-law of the Court supports a right for individuals and associations to be able to freely determine

---

64   *Moscow Branch of the Salvation Army v. Russia*, op.cit., para 92.

what symbols and what clothing their beliefs require of them and a prima facie right to display them both in public and in private. This view is further reinforced by the way in which Article 9 expressly links worship, practice teaching and observance with public as well as private acts. The idea of 'observance', in particular, includes forms of religiously inspired acts such as parades, etc, which are intrinsically public in their nature. Moreover, the clear recognition that activities intended to encourage a change of religion through teaching, proclamation, public worship, etc, are also legitimate forms of manifesting beliefs once again clearly locates the practice of religion in an open as opposed to a closed environment. Given that organisations are entitled to determine the proper forms of organisation and of dress for adherents, it would amount to an intrusion into the internal life of the organisation, as well as being a limitation of the freedom of the individual to manifest their religion or belief, to seek to restrict the public display of religious symbols and clothing in situations which are clearly foreseen by the Convention as having an intrinsically public dimension.

(C) Non-discrimination in the Enjoyment of the Rights

A third principle is that of non-discrimination and is derived from a number of separate, though interlocking, strands which will be looked at in turn.

(a) ECHR Article 14

The first of these strands is Article 14 of the Convention which provides that:

> 'The enjoyment of the rights and freedoms set forth in this Convention shall be secured without discrimination on any ground such as sex, race, colour, language, religion, political or other opinion, national or social origin, association with a national minority, property, birth or other status'.

As is well known, Article 14 'has no independent existence' and has effect 'solely in relation to the "enjoyment of the rights and freedoms" safeguarded by these provisions'. At the same time, it is not necessary for there to have been an actual breach of another Convention provision in order for there to have been a breach of Article 14: otherwise, all that Article 14 would do is add a second violation to the first, rather than extending the scope of protection. What is needed is a nexus between the alleged discriminatory act and a Convention right. As the Court put it in *Abdulaziz, Cabales and Balkandali v. the United Kingdom*, 'Although the application of Article 14 does not necessarily presuppose a breach of those provisions – and to this extent is autonomous – there can be no room for its application unless the facts at issue fall within the ambit of one or more of the latter.'[65] It may well be that the facts not only suggest that there has been a violation of a substantive right but that the violation was also discriminatory in nature and so might also give rise to a violation of Article 14 in conjunction with Article 9. In many cases in which there has been both a violation of Article 9 and discriminatory treatment, there is something of a 'choice' as to whether the gist of the case is so closely connected with one of these aspects that a finding of a violation under that one heading renders it unnecessary to consider the other. It is not necessary to pursue this further here, but there will also be cases in which both elements are so in evidence as to justify finding a violation under both the substantive Article and Article 14.

The first question to be asked, then, is whether the alleged discriminatory behaviour falls within the ambit – within the scope – of a Convention right. If it does, the next question is whether a similarly situated group has been treated in a more favourable fashion. Finally, if this is indeed the case, the final question to be asked is whether there this difference in treatment is justified: the Court has said that a difference in treatment is discriminatory if it 'has no objective and reasonable justification', that is if it does not pursue a 'legitimate aim' or if there is not a 'reasonable relationship of proportionality' between the means employed and the aim sought to be realised.

As regards the freedom of religion or belief, the first question becomes whether the matter at issue is an exercise of that freedom. In the early case of *Choudhury* v. *the United Kingdom*, the Commission decided that the freedom to manifest religion or belief in worship, teaching, practice or observance did not embrace a right to see actions brought for blas-

> When it comes to discrimination regarding the freedom of religion or beliefs, there can be no room for the application of Article 14 unless the facts at issue fall within the ambit of Article 9.

---

65   *Abdulaziz, Cabales and Balkandali v. the United Kingdom*, judgment of 28 May 1985, Series A no. 94, para 71.

phemy and so even though such actions were only available in respect of Anglican Christianity and not in respect of the Islamic faith, such discrimination fell outside the ambit of Article 9 with the result that there could be no question of its giving rise to an issue under Article 14.[66] If however, the state offers a protection which goes beyond what the minimum requirements of substantive rights require, then that too comes within the ambit of the right. It has already been seen that the requirement to offer minimum protection to the sensibilities of believers means that such protections as are offered should be non-discriminatory in nature.

The emergence of the principle of 'respect' as a substantive aspect of the right, as outlined above, takes this further and suggests that any state-sponsored activities which potentially cast a negative light over a particular form of religion or belief would fall within the ambit of Article 9 and so need to be justified in order to avoid violating Article 14. The *Case of 97 Members of the Gldani Congregation of Jehovah's Witnesses and 4 Others v. Georgia* illustrates the coming together of these principles. In that case the supporters of a radical priest of the Orthodox Church in Georgia, Father Basil, had been involved in violently disrupting a service of worship by members of the Jehovah's Witnesses, resulting, inter alia, in serious physical injuries to a considerable number of the congregation. The evidence showed that the authorities had not intervened to try to prevent this from occurring, nor had they properly investigated or taken action against those involved, and so the responsibility of the state was engaged. Similar incidents had subsequently occurred, involving other faith communities as well as the Jehovah's Witnesses. There was no doubt that the facts showed there to have been a violation of Article 9, since there had been an unjustified interference with the exercise of the freedom of religion. The Court framed that finding in the following fashion:

> 'the Court considers that, through their inactivity, the relevant authorities failed in their duty to take the necessary measures to ensure that the group of Orthodox extremists led by Father Basil tolerated the existence of the applicants' religious community and enabled them to exercise freely their rights to freedom of religion.'[67]

---

66   *Choudhury v. the United Kingdom*, op.cit.

67   *Case of 97 Members of the Gldani Congregation of Jehovah's Witnesses and Others v. Georgia*, no. 71156/01, para 134, ECHR 2007-

We shall return to the question of the duty of the state later, but at this point it should be stressed that the finding of a violation was presented in terms of the state's overall failure to maintain a climate of toleration and of respect (though that word was not used) for the rights of others. Against this background, there will almost always be a powerful argument concerning the discriminatory behaviour of the state in the exercise of its obligation under the Convention and, in this case, the Court did indeed decide that there had been a violation of Article 14 in conjunction with Article 9 in addition to the violation of Article 9 itself. In a passage worth quoting at length, the Court said that:

> 140. ... in the instant case, the refusal by the police to intervene promptly at the scene of the incident in order to protect the applicants ... from acts of religiously-motivated violence, and the subsequent indifference shown towards the applicants by the relevant authorities, was to a large extent the corollary of the applicants' religious convictions. The Government has not adduced any counter-arguments. In the Court's opinion, the comments and attitude of the state employees who were alerted about the attack or subsequently instructed to conduct the relevant investigation cannot be considered compatible with the principle of equality of every person before the law .... No justification for this discriminatory treatment in respect of the applicants has been put forward by the Government.

> 141. The Court considers that the negligent attitude towards extremely serious unlawful acts, shown by the police and the investigation authorities by the police on account of the applicants' faith, enabled Father Basil to continue to advocate hatred through the media and to pursue acts of religiously-motivated violence, accompanied by his supporters, while alleging that the latter enjoyed the unofficial support of the authorities ... .

Not only was there a clear violation of Article 9 but there was also sufficient evidence to support the conclusion that the state, through its tacit support for the violence used against the applicants, was treating them in a discriminatory fashion.

(b) Positive obligations

A second strand of development concerning non-discrimination in the enjoyment of the freedom of religion or belief
concerns positive obligations and both flows from, and
is illustrated by, the judgment of the Court in the case of
Thlimmenos v. Greece. This case concerned a Jehovah's Witness who had been convicted because of his unwillingness
to wear a military uniform and serve in the armed forces.
Some years later he passed the examinations necessary to
become a Chartered Accountant but was barred from being able to do so because of his having this prior criminal
conviction. The Government argued that this was a rule
of general application which served the public interest
whereas the applicant argued that the law ought to distinguish between those convicted of offences committed as a
result of their manifesting their religion or belief and those
convicted of other offences. The Court pointed out that
whilst a violation of Article 14 occurred when states treat
differently persons in analogous situations without providing an objective and reasonable justification, it was not
limited to such situations. It said that:

> 'The right not to be discriminated against in the enjoy-
> ment of the rights guaranteed under the Convention is also
> violated when states without an objective and reasonable
> justification fail to treat differently persons whose situations
> are significantly different.'[68]

The Court felt that those convicted for offences related to
the manifestation of their beliefs might indeed be a different
situation from those convicted for other reasons. It argued
that 'a conviction for refusing on religious or philosophical grounds to wear the military uniform cannot imply
any dishonesty or moral turpitude likely to undermine the
offender's ability to exercise this profession. Excluding the
applicant on the ground that he was an unfit person was
not, therefore, justified.'[69]

The significance of this approach for questions concerning
the wearing of religious symbols is evident. Should there be
a generalised restriction on the wearing of any particular

---

68   *Thlimmenos v. Greece* [GC], no. 34369/97, para 44, ECHR 2000-
     IV.

69   *Ibid*, para. 47.

type of clothing or symbol which is of religious significance to some but not to all, it will raise the question of whether the state is responsible for a failure to 'treat differently persons whose situations are significantly different'. Should this be the case, there will be a violation of Article 14 in conjunction with Article 9 unless an objective and reasonable justification can be given.

(c)　Protocol No. 12

A third strand of development relates to Protocol No. 12 to the European Convention on Human Rights[70] which was adopted in 2000 and entered into force on 1 April 2005. At the time of writing, 17 of the 47 Member states of the Council of Europe have ratified the Protocol and so are bound by it, these being: Albania, Andorra, Armenia, Bosnia and Herzegovina, Croatia, Cyprus, Finland, Georgia, Luxembourg, Montenegro, The Netherlands, Romania, San Marino, Serbia, Spain, the Former Yugoslav Republic of Macedonia and the Ukraine. A further 20 states have signed but have yet to ratify the Protocol.

Article 1 of the Protocol provides that:

'1.　The enjoyment of any right set forth by law shall be secured without discrimination on any ground such as sex, race, colour, language, religion, political or other opinion, national or social origin, association with a national minority, property, birth or other status.

2.　No one shall be discriminated against by any public authority on any ground such as those mentioned in paragraph 1.'

This moves beyond Article 14 by removing the need for a nexus with another substantive convention right, replacing this with a right not to be subjected to discrimination in the enjoyment of any right 'set forth by law', whether national or international in origins. The idea of 'set forth by law' embraces not only legislative provisions but also rights inferred from obligations under national law, by the exercise of discretionary powers or by other acts of omissions attributable to a public authority.

70　CETS no. 177.

To the extent that the wearing of religious clothing and symbols represents a manifestation of religion and so is within the ambit of Article 9 such discrimination is already addressed by Article 14 and so Protocol 12 adds little to the protections which are already in place. However, Protocol 12 does offer a residual protection for unusual situations which, for whatever reason, might fall beyond the ambit of Article 9. In such circumstances, this more general 'equality' provision would come into play and offer a degree of protection to religious believers against discriminatory treatment which was attributable to public authorities in ratifying states.

(D) Living Instrument

A final overarching principle should also be highlighted and although it may be dealt with briefly it is of considerable importance. The Court has stressed on numerous occasions that the Convention is a 'living' instrument' which is to be interpreted in the light of present day conditions. As a result the Court cannot but be influenced by the developments and commonly accepted standards operable within member states of the Council of Europe and, drawing on this approach, the Court has said that 'the increasingly high standard being required in the area of the protection of human rights and fundamental liberties correspondingly and inevitably requires greater firmness in assessing breaches of the fundamental values of democratic societies'.[71]

Two important points flow from this. First, the Convention is not static and through the processes of interpretation and application it is capable of evolving to address newly emergent concerns or to reappraise existing approaches in the light of new insights into the nature of the democratic societies which it addresses. Secondly, and as an inevitable corollary, the approaches set out in the Court's jurisprudence are not immutable but are open to re-appraisal over time. This is particularly true in areas in which states have traditionally enjoyed a considerable margin of appreciation, including the freedom of religion or belief, since the emergence of a common European approach would have the effect of limiting its breadth and be a precursor to the emergence of a Convention-wide normative approach. It

> The Court has stressed on numerous occasions that the Convention is a 'living instrument' which is to be interpreted in the light of present-day conditions.

---

71   *Selmouni v. France* [GC], no. 25803/94, para 101, ECHR 1999-V.

may well be that the 'living instrument' principal might provide a conceptual means through which the Convention can respond to the increasing interest in, and importance of, the manifestation of religion and belief within the democratic societies of the Council of Europe.

#IV   The Role and Responsibilities of the State

The previous section identified a number of key conceptual principles which underpin the approach to the freedom of religion and belief within the Convention framework. Some of these were specific to Article 9, others were of a more general nature but which had a particular relevance for the realisation of that freedom. This section continues the theme of identifying core strands in the approach of the Court to the freedom of religion or belief but, rather than looking at more general and overarching principles, it looks at how those principles work themselves out in practice.

This section identifies core strands in the approach of the Court to the freedom of religion or belief by examining how the following principles work in practice: (a) neutrality and impartiality; (b) fostering pluralism and tolerance; (c) protecting the rights and freedoms of others.

(A)   Neutrality and Impartiality

There has been a subtle, but significant, shift in the perception of the role of the state in relation to the freedom of religion and belief. We have already seen that the individual rights approach outlined in section II has been developed by the principle of 'respect' and by the recognition of the communal aspects of the rights as outlined in Section III. Whilst approaching Article 9 from the perspective of an individual works well when an individual is challenging the manner in which the state has acted in relation to their personal enjoyment of a particular aspect of that right, it works less well in situations in which what is really at stake is the approach of the state either to religion or belief generally or to a particular form of religion or belief. In recent times, the Court has increasingly been called on to consider cases of this nature and, indeed, a number of the cases previously considered from the perspective of the 'individual' might in reality be best viewed from this more community oriented perspective.

The response of the Court, echoing the principle of respect, has been to call on the state to act in a neutral fashion as between religions and as between religious and non

The response of the Court, echoing the principle of respect, has been to call on the state to act in a neutral fashion as between religions and as between religious and non-religious forms of belief.

religious forms of belief. In *Hasan and Chaush* v. *Bulgaria*, for example, it emphasised that the role of the state was not to 'take sides' by endorsing one religious community at the expense of another but was to act in an even-handed fashion, concluding that 'a failure by the authorities to remain neutral in the exercise of their powers .... must lead to the conclusion that the state interfered with the believers' freedom to manifest their religion'.[1] Unsurprisingly, the same approach has been taken in cases which have been brought not by individuals but by religious communities themselves. The leading case remains that of the *Metropolitan Church of Bessarabia v. Moldova*, which concerned the refusal of the Moldovan authorities to grant official recognition to the applicant Church which had the practical effect of making both the Church as an organisation and the religious activities of its adherents unlawful. The Court said that 'in exercising its regulatory power in this sphere and in its relations with the various religions, denominations and beliefs, the state has a duty to remain neutral and impartial'.[2] The duty to remain neutral and impartial has now been re-iterated on many occasions and it is clear that any evidence that the state has failed to act in such a fashion in its dealings with religious bodies will require justification under Article 9(2) if it is not to amount to a breach of Article 9.

This duty has a number of facets, perhaps the most important being that 'the state's duty of neutrality and impartiality is incompatible with any power on the state's part to assess the legitimacy of religious beliefs or the ways in which they are expressed'.[3] This is of particular importance for issues concerning religious clothing and religious symbols since it underscores the need to permit individuals themselves to determine whether the wearing or display of any particular items is of religious significance to them, and the state will be in breach of its duty of neutrality and impartiality if it imposes its interpretation of their significance at the expense of that of the believer.

So far, the case-law considered has established that the state must remain neutral and impartial when it has deal-

---

1   *Hasan and Chaush v. Bulgaria* [GC], op.cit., para 78.

2   *Metropolitan Church of Bessarabia and Others v. Moldova*, op.cit., para 116.

3   *Manoussakis and Others v. Greece*, judgment of 26 September 1996, *Reports of Judgments and Decisions* 1996-IV, para. 47.

ings with religious believers and religious organisations. In some cases, however, the Court has gone even further and suggested that states are under a variety of positive obligations with regard to the freedom of religion and belief and in the case of *Leyla Şahin v. Turkey* it referred to its having 'frequently emphasised the state's role as the neutral and impartial organiser of the exercise of various religions, faiths and beliefs'.[4] Just as cases such as *Kokkinakis* and *Larrisis* emphasised that the role of the state was to ensure that there was a 'level playing field' between believers (and between believers and non-believers), so it was that in *Leyla Şahin* the Court saw the role of the state as being to ensure that this was the case *ab initio* by emphasising the state's responsibilities as the neutral and impartial *organiser* of the exercise of religions, faiths and beliefs. This puts the state in a rather different position from that which it previously occupied. Rather than being required to ensure that it remains neutral and impartial in its dealings with religions and with believers, its role becomes one of ensuring that religious life within the state is neutral and impartial, which is a subtle, but important difference.

> The state's duty of neutrality and impartiality is incompatible with any power on the state's part to assess the legitimacy of religious beliefs or the ways in which they are expressed.

This can play out in a number of different ways. Neutrality and impartiality means that the state ought to have no interest in internal organisational issues unless the results are such as to endanger the public order, health, morals or the rights and freedoms of others. Short of this, it should refrain from engaging with internal affairs, thus reinforcing the principle of autonomy. For example, in the case of *Serif v. Greece*, the Court said that 'in democratic societies the state does not need to take measures to ensure that religious communities are brought under a unified leadership'.[5] Such an approach casts the role of the state as a 'facilitator' of organisational and individual religious freedom. It is enough if believers are able to function as a religious community within the state in a manner which allows them, as believers, the rights which flow from Article 9 and, of course, Article 14 of the ECHR.

An alternative model – and the now dominant model – takes a different approach, emphasising the responsibility of the state to ensure the realisation of all convention rights and, drawing on the key statement of principle in the *Kokki-*

---

4   *Leyla Şahin v. Turkey* [GC], op.cit., para 107.

5   *Serif v. Greece*, no 38178/97, para 52, ECHR 1999-IX.

nakis case, emphasising the need for the freedom of religion and belief to be seen and understood in the broader context of democratic society. In the *Kokkinakis* case the Court said that 'the freedom of thought, conscience and religion is one of the foundations of a "democratic Society" ... the pluralism indissociable from a democratic society ... depends on it'. It also said that 'in democratic societies ... it may be necessary to place restrictions on this freedom in order to reconcile the interests of the various groups and ensure that everyone's beliefs are respected'.[6] On the one hand, this offers a recognition of the public value of the freedom of religion and belief and means that when exercising its role as the 'neutral and impartial organiser' of religious life the state does so in a fashion which respects and reflects this. On the other hand, it emphasises the extent to which it is legitimate for the state to allow the broader needs of society to impact upon the activities of religious bodies and believers in order to secure a proper balance between the rights of all within the broader community which comprises the democratic society as a whole. When combined with the newly emergent responsibility of the state, the goals of neutrality and impartiality become clear, these being the fostering of pluralism and tolerance and the protection of the rights and freedoms of others, both of which will now be looked at in a little more detail.

(B) Fostering Pluralism and Tolerance

The application of the principles already identified will have the practical effect of fostering a climate of pluralism and tolerance. If, for example, the state is to remain neutral in its dealings with religious organisations and with believers, not express any preference for, or pass comment upon, any particular form of belief, respect the internal autonomy of not only individuals but of belief communities as well (to the extent that this is compatible with the rights and freedoms of others), ensure that there is a 'level playing field' and, whilst doing all of this, be animated by an overarching principle of 'respect' for the beliefs of others – then it is difficult to see how this can fail to help foster a climate of pluralism and tolerance. However, the Court sees the fostering of pluralism and tolerance as more than an 'incidental outcome' but as a goal which is to be achieved by

---

6   *Kokkinakis v. Greece*, op.cit., paras. 31 and 33.

the application of the principles and approaches which have already been identified.

This raises some difficult and delicate issues. Most religious belief systems advance truth claims which are, in varying degrees, absolutist in nature and reject at least elements of the validity of others. In addition, the need to allow for the 'market place' of ideas requires that there be exchanges of views, expressions of beliefs, ideas and opinions and forms of manifestation which may be unwelcome and, perhaps, offensive, to others. This is both necessary for the realisation of pluralism and tolerance yet at the same time runs the risk of compromising it. We have already seen that the Court expects believers to cope with a fairly high degree of challenge to their systems of belief in the pursuit of the more general goals of securing pluralism and tolerance: in the *Otto-Preminger-Institut* case, for example, the Court said that:

> 'Those who choose to exercise the freedom to manifest their religion .... cannot reasonably expect to be exempt from all criticism. They must tolerate and accept the denial by others of their religious beliefs and even the propagation by others of doctrines hostile to their faith'.[7]

Whilst respect for the freedom of religion and belief cannot require others to respect the doctrines and teachings of faith traditions other than one's own (if any) it can, and does, require that one be respectful of them. The role of the state in such cases is to ensure that the believer, or non-believer, is able to continue to enjoy their convention rights, albeit that they may be troubled or disturbed by what they see and hear around them. As the *Otto-Preminger-Institut* case itself suggests, it is only when the manner in which the views, ideas or opinions are expressed are akin to a 'malicious violation of the spirit of tolerance'[8] that it is for the state to intervene.

This approach has been reflected in a variety of other situations. For example, in the case of *Serif v. Greece* the applicant argued that his freedom of religion had been violated by his being convicted to assuming the functions of the leader of the Muslim community in Rodopi, the leadership

The role of the state is to ensure that the believer, or non-believer, is able to continue to enjoy their convention rights, albeit that they may be troubled or disturbed by what they see and hear around them.

---

7   *Otto-Preminger Institut v. Austria*, op.cit., para 47.

8   *Ibid.*

of which was in dispute. The Court said that 'Although [it] recognises that it is possible that tension is created in situations where a religious or any other community becomes divided, it considers that this is one of the unavoidable consequences of pluralism. The role of the authorities in such circumstances is not to remove the cause of tension by eliminating pluralism, but to ensure that the competing groups tolerate each other'.[9] Taken at face value, this approach is not unproblematic since it suggests that the state is not only entitled but may be required to exercise a form of oversight over the internal life of religious communities in the interests of ensuring pluralism and tolerance. At the same time, it is not the role of the state to 'step in' and 'sort out' the problem since doing so would not only fail to respect the principle of autonomy but would also fail to demonstrate the degree of neutrality and impartiality which the state must show in its dealings with believers. Balancing these concerns – the need to promote pluralism and tolerance whilst respecting the beliefs and autonomy (personal and organisational) of others is a delicate task and can be approached in a number of ways.

For example, in the case of the *Metropolitan Church of Bessarabia v. Moldova* the Government had argued that by recognizing the Applicant church as a legal entity it would be broadening the rift within the Orthodox community and that the impartial response to the situation would be to encourage the applicant church to 'settle it's differences with the already recognised church from which it wishes to split'.[10] The Court rejected this argument, saying that 'the state's duty of neutrality ... is incompatible with any power ... to assess the legitimacy of religious beliefs, and requires the state to ensure that conflicting groups tolerate each other, even when they originated in the same group. In the present case ... [by] taking the view that the new group was not a new denomination and making its recognition depend on the will of an ecclesiastical authority that had been recognised ... the Government failed to discharge their duty'.[11] One can see the force of both arguments. However, the former argument views the role of the state as being ultimately passive in nature – avoiding conduct which gives

---

9   *Serif v. Greece*, op.cit., para 53.
10   *Metropolitan Church of Bessarabia and Others v. Moldova*, op.cit., para 123.
11   *Idem*.

the appearance of endorsing a particular form of religion or belief, the validity of which is contested by others. This fails to do justice to the more activist approach to the promotion of pluralism and tolerance which the Court has called for, although this too may operate in a variety of directions. In the *Metropolitan Church* case, the promotion of pluralism seems to have been given enhanced weight when construing the content of the obligation to ensure that 'conflicting groups tolerate each other' and the result seeks to support the presence of varied and diverse bodies of thought co-existing and interacting with each other within the broader political community. This might be contrasted with the case of *the Supreme Holy Council of the Muslim Community v. Bulgaria*, in which the Court placed more emphasis on the role of the state as the promoter of tolerance. In that case the Court, whilst re-iterating that the state should not favour a particular leader or faction within a divided community, also commented that the state was 'under a constitutional duty to secure religious tolerance and peaceful relations between groups of believers' (which it did not find objectionable) and that ' ... discharging it may require engaging in mediation. Neutral mediation between groups of believers would not in principle amount to state interference with the believers' rights ..., although the state authorities must be cautious in this particularly delicate area'.[12]

These comments relate to the role of the state in respect of internal matters of religious organisations and they suggest that the positive elements of the state's duty to promote tolerance and pluralism may permit it to work alongside such bodies in order to realise those objectives. In other words, neutrality and impartiality does not mean that the state must distance itself from religion and religious bodies. On the contrary, it suggests that the state may engage with them on a non-partisan basis in order to assist in the realisation of these goals.

There are implications for the wearing of religious symbols which flow from this more dynamic approach to fostering pluralism and tolerance. It has already been seen that the pursuit of pluralism means that believers may have to be exposed to ideas and arguments which they may find personally unpalatable. It also means that believers must

---

12   *Supreme Holy Council of the Muslim Community v. Bulgaria*,
      op.cit., para 77.

accept the legitimacy of there being a divergence of views on matters of fundamental significance to them within the broader society of which they form a part. The pursuit of tolerance implies that believers must accept the legitimacy of this diversity as a necessary consequence of there being a flourishing democratic society and it falls to the state to ensure that this is the case, limited only by what is necessary to protect the rights and freedoms of others. This, of course, works in both directions and it is equally applicable to non-believers who are faced with the manifestation of forms of belief which they might find unwelcome or unpalatable and which might include the presence of religious symbols in the public space. In such situations, the same goal of fostering pluralism and tolerance would apply and, drawing on the words on the Court in *Serif v. Greece* (and repeated on numerous occasions since) the role of the state is not to remove the cause of tension by eliminating pluralism, but through its actions seek to ensure toleration.

(C)   Protecting the Rights and Freedoms of Others

In both *the Metropolitan Church of Bessarabia* case and in the case of the *97 Members of the Gladini Congregation* cases the Court made it clear that 'neutrality' and 'impartiality' cannot be used to justify a failure to protect the rights of believers under Article 9. Likewise, cases such as *Otto-Preminger-Institut v. Austria* show that the need to foster pluralism and tolerance cannot be used to justify such failings either. The point at which the limits of state abstention in the interests of neutrality and impartiality and state intrusion in the interests of fostering pluralism and tolerance are re-connected is in the overarching need to protect the rights and freedoms of others, believers and non-believers, both within religious bodies and within the broader political community. This, of course, take us back to the limitations on the enjoyment of the right permitted on the basis of Article 9(2) and which can only be determined on a case-by-case basis.

Later sections of this Manual will look in detail at how the Court has conducted this exercise as regards the wearing of religious symbols. It is, however, appropriate to identify at this point a particular aspect of this balancing exercise which, although usually addressed within the framework of Article 9(2) as a legitimate ground of restriction, is better

> The point at which the limits of state abstention in the interests of neutrality and impartiality and state intrusion in the interests of fostering pluralism and tolerance are re-connected is in the overarching need to protect the rights and freedoms of others, believers and non-believers.

seen as a reflection of a more overarching goal – this being
the protection of the general rights and freedoms of others through the preservation of the democratic nature of
the state. This sets the 'outer limits' of what neutrality and
impartiality and the promotion of pluralism and tolerance
might require of a state and of a society. We have already
noted that Article 15 permits states to derogate from Convention rights in times of national emergency threatening
the life of the nation, and that Article 17 requires that convention rights are not used to undermine the rights of others. Our concern at this point is with sets of circumstances
in which it is argued that, by their actions, individuals or
organisations are negatively impacting upon the democratic
framework which the Convention is to uphold.

In the case of the *Metropolitan Church of Bessarabia* v.
Moldova the government argued that its refusal to register
the applicant church was justified on the grounds of preserving the territorial integrity of the state, maintaining that
recognition would 'revive old Russo-Romanian rivalries
within the population, thus endangering social stability and
even Moldova's territorial integrity'.[13] The Court accepted
that this was a 'legitimate aim' for the purposes of Article
9(2) in that it sought to protect public order and public
safety, although it decided that no evidence has been presented which supported such a conclusion. Such claims are
likely to be rare – though there are echoes of this approach
in the case of the *Moscow Branch of the Salvation Army v.
Russia*, where the Court, noted that although the applicant's
members wore military style uniforms, on the evidence
presented 'It could not seriously be maintained that the applicant branch advocated a violent change of constitutional
foundations or thereby undermined the integrity or security
of the state'.[14] Where there is such evidence, however,
there can be little doubt that the state would be entitled to
restrict the activities of believers to the extent necessary to
address the risk.

The Court has said on numerous occasions that democracy
is the only political model compatible with the Convention
and in a series of cases concerning Article 11 (the freedom
of association) the Court has also made it clear that it is

---

13   *Metropolitan Church of Bessarabia and Others v. Moldova*, op.cit.,
     para 111.
14   *Moscow Branch of the Salvation Army v. Russia*, op.cit., para 92.

entitled to act in order to preserve the integrity and proper functioning of the internal democratic structures of the state. However, the threshold for such intervention is high. Thus in a series of cases the Court rejected claims by Turkey that it had been entitled to ban political parties whose policies were allegedly antithetical to Turkish democracy, arguing that:

> 'The fact that such a political project is considered incompatible with the current principles and structures of the Turkish state does not mean that it infringes democratic rules. It is of the essence of democracy to allow diverse political projects to be proposed and debated, even those that call into question the way in which a state is currently organised, provided that they do not harm democracy itself.'[15]

In the case of *Refah Partisi v. Turkey*, the Court addressed a situation in which a political party whose policies embraced aspects of Islamic thought and which had been a partner in Government was dissolved, primarily on the grounds that prominent members of the party had called for the introduction of elements of Shar'ia law which, it was claimed, would be incompatible with the principle of secularism which undergirded Turkish democracy. For the avoidance of any doubt, the Court confirmed that a 'political party animated by the moral values imposed by a religion cannot be regarded as intrinsically inimical to the fundamental principles of democracy, as set forth in the Convention'[16] and recalled that in its previous case-law it had said that 'there can be no justification for hindering a political group solely because it seeks to debate in public the situation of part of the state's population and to take part in the nation's political life in order to find, according to democratic rules, solutions capable of satisfying everyone concerned'.[17] This, then, highlights the fact that religious believers and religious communities are to be welcomed as participants in the public life of the state, including participation in the democratic process should they wish to do so.

---

15 *Socialist Party of Turkey (STP) and Others v. Turkey*, no 26482/95, para 47, 12 November 2003 (emphasis added).

16 *Refah Partisi (the Welfare Party) and Others v. Turkey* [GC], op.cit., para 100.

17 *Ibid*, para 97, quoting *Case of Freedom and Democracy Party (ÖZDEP) v. Turkey* [GC]. no. 23885/94, para 57, ECHR 1999-VIII.

In the *Refah Partisi* case the Court also said that 'a political party may promote a change in the law or the legal
and constitutional structures of the state on two conditions: firstly, the means used to that end must be legal and
democratic; secondly, the change proposed must itself
be compatible with fundamental democratic principles'.[18]
These two propositions will be considered separately. The
first proposition is unproblematic since it merely confirms
that, in common with all other participants in the democratic process, the religiously motivated participation in
public life must respect the principles of democratic governance. For example, the Court has said, 'a political party
whose leaders incite to violence or put forward a policy
which fails to respect democracy or which is aimed at the
destruction of democracy and the flouting of the rights and
freedoms recognised in a democracy cannot lay claim to
the Convention's protection against penalties imposed on
those grounds'.[19] It has also made it clear that 'The freedoms
guaranteed by Article 11, and by Articles 9 and 10 of the
Convention, cannot deprive the authorities of a state in
which an association, through its activities, jeopardises that
state's institutions, of the right to protect those institutions'.

The Court's second proposition in the *Refah Partisi* case
raises the slightly different point of whether such participation must respect what might be called the 'culture' of a
particular democratic polity. Where that change in culture
may be such as to undermine the essence of that particular polity, the answer is once again clear and, in the case
of religious groups, the Court has noted that 'in the past
political movements based on religious fundamentalism
have been able to seize political power in certain states and
have had the opportunity to set up the model of society
which they had in mind. It considers that, in accordance
with the Convention's provisions, each Contracting state
may oppose such political movements in the light of its
historical experience'. It is not to be assumed, however, that
every religiously inspired political platform will necessarily
be of a fundamentalist nature and have such an influence or
impact and the more difficult question is whether the state
is entitled to act in order to buttress elements of its foun-

---

18   *Refah Partisi (the Welfare Party) and* Others *v. Turkey* [GC],
     op.cit., para 98.

19   *Yazar* and others *v. Turkey*, no. 22723/93, 22724/93 and 22725/93,
     para 49, ECHR 2002-II.

dational assumptions where they are challenged through
a democratic process in a fashion which neither threatens
the integrity of the democratic system or runs the risk of
imposing extremism on others, but which nevertheless offer a substantially different vision of the nature of the state,
from which legislative consequences would inevitably flow.
In the case of Turkey the Court has said that 'the principle
of secularism is certainly one of the fundamental principles
of the state which are in harmony with the rule of law and
respect for human rights and democracy'[20] and so, therefore, it thought that Turkey was entitled to take a range of
measures – including placing restrictions on the wearing
of religious clothing and the display of religious symbols
– which it, Turkey, considered to be necessary to preserve
that element of the political culture of Turkish democracy
– provided, always, that those restrictions were legitimate
and proportionate under Article 9(2).

This same approach has also been taken to uphold the
ethos of state-run institutions which, it is presumed, can
legitimately be expected to exemplify the same overarching
principles. The case of *Leyla Şahin* v. *Turkey*, for example,
concerned the legitimacy of a ban on the wearing of Islamic
headscarves in a state-run university in Turkey, a ban which
had been upheld by the Constitutional Court. The Court
observed that:[21]

> 'it is the principle of secularism, as elucidated by the Con-
> stitutional Court (see paragraph 39 above), which is the
> paramount consideration underlying the ban on the wearing
> of religious symbols in universities. In such a context, where
> the values of pluralism, respect for the rights of others and,
> in particular, equality before the law of men and women are
> being taught and applied in practice, it is understandable that
> the relevant authorities should wish to preserve the secular
> nature of the institution concerned and so consider it con-
> trary to such values to allow religious attire, including, as in
> the present case, the Islamic headscarf, to be worn.'

This case will be considered in more detail later, but at this
point it may be used to illustrate the point that the state is
entitled to look to the character of its institutions as well as

---

20   *Refah Partisi (the Welfare Party) and* Others *v. Turkey* [GC],
     op.cit., para 93.
21   *Leyla Şahin v. Turkey* [GC], op.cit., para 116.

to the functioning of its democratic system and ensure that they are consonant with the national ethos. It is important to emphasise however, that the Court has not said in these cases that either the state or state-run institutions must be secular in nature. It has said that since secularism is compatible with pluralism and democracy it is legitimate for a state to project a secularist ethos whilst respecting the rights and freedoms of others. It has *not* said that secularism is the *only* concept of governance which is compatible with pluralism and democracy. Indeed, were it to do so, it would not only call into question the legitimacy of the state Churches which are to be found in a number of member states of the Council of Europe but it would also run the risk of falling foul of its own jurisprudence by privileging one form of belief system – secularism- at the expense of others. This might be difficult to reconcile with its role of exercising judicial oversight of the manner in which states fulfil the role of the neutral and impartial organiser of religion and belief.

It might be concluded that whilst the state remains free to determine its guiding organisational principles and whilst it remains open to the state to take steps to preserve the nature of its democracy and associated institutions, it may only do so in pursuit of Convention aims of democratic governance informed by pluralism and tolerance. Likewise, those who engage in public life and life in the 'public square', including believers and belief communities, may do so on the condition that they respect the principles of democracy and human rights, of tolerance and pluralism.

Pluralism, secularism, respect of the rights of others, and gender equality are important values taken into account by the Court when examining restrictions to the wearing of religious symbols.

#V The Role and Responsibilities of Individuals and Religious Communities

Having looked at the role and responsibilities of the state, we can consider the role and responsibilities of individuals and of belief communities quite quickly since they are largely the natural corollaries of what has already been said. There are, however, a number of points which need to be stressed, and which flow from their different relationship to the right as set out in the Convention. Simply stated, the individual and religious or belief communities are the beneficiaries of the right and not its guarantor. Thus whilst it is the responsibility of the state to ensure the full enjoyment of that right to all who are subject to their jurisdiction, the responsibilities of the individual are chiefly to ensure that in their enjoyment of that right they do not abuse the freedom which it offers. The legitimacy of the various limitations on the manifestation of the freedom of religion or belief may ultimately all be traced back to an assessment of whether or not this is the case.

The Court has frequently said that the freedom of religion and belief is primarily a matter of individual conscience. The absolute nature of the *'forum internum'*, the sphere of personal belief, means that the overarching principles identified in the previous section and which guide the state are not directly applicable to the individual and to the religious community in the same fashion. Thus it is not necessary for them to be neutral and impartial in their dealings with others, nor is it for them to *foster* pluralism and tolerance – though it is of course necessary that they accept a pluralist approach and display tolerance in the context of the plural society of which they form a part. Similarly, it is not the role of individuals and religious organisations to seek to 'protect' the rights of others in the Convention sense of the terms, though they may of course seek to vindicate their own rights and freedoms though its processes.

Individuals and belief communities should conduct themselves in a fashion which respects the structures and systems of pluralist democracy, the Convention itself, the rights and freedoms of others and which honours the particular obligation to show proper respect for the objects of religious veneration of others.

Ultimately, then, what the Convention expects is that individuals and belief communities should conduct themselves in a fashion which respects the structures and systems of pluralist democracy, respects the Convention itself, is properly respectful of the rights and freedoms of others and, which honours the particular obligation to show proper respect for the objects of religious veneration of others. It should be clear that these are the same expectations which apply to everyone touched by the Convention system.

The Wearing of Religious Symbols in Public Areas: Definitional Issues

Having set out the Convention framework relevant to the wearing of religious symbols in public areas, we are now in a position to look at a number of definitional issues which need to be addressed before that framework can be applied to the subject matter of this Manual, these being: 'what is a 'religious symbol'? what is meant by the 'wearing' of religious symbols'? and 'what is a 'public area'? The following sections will look at each of these questions but it needs to be stressed at the outset that these terms cannot be understood in isolation from each other and, indeed, from the broader context of Article 9.

(A) The 'Visibility' of Religions and Beliefs in Public Life and in the Public Sphere

Whilst the issue of wearing religious symbols in public areas is clearly a contentious issue, it is very important to realise that it is merely a sub-set of a more general question concerning what might be termed the 'visibility of religion' and it is necessary to explore this a little in order to avoid making errors when looking at the key terms which define the scope of this Manual. For example, it is clearly the case that not all of the things which are of symbolic significance to religious believers are things which can be worn or displayed, even when they concern what might be called the 'public space'. To take an extreme example, the underlying issue in the cases such as *Stedman v. the United Kingdom*[1] and *Casimiro v. Luxembourg*[2] is not so much the narrow question of whether the applicants have the right to avoid working or schooling on their holy days but the more general question of the special significance of those days to believers being recognised by the State. state recognition of

---

1   *Stedman v. the United Kingdom,* op.cit.
2   *Casimiro* v. *Luxembourg* (dec.), op.cit.

the special status of a religious day or festival can be seen as
having symbolic status. However, the symbolism here is not
the symbolism *of* the religion but a symbolic statement by
the state regarding the *status* of the religion.

Some see this as tantamount to state endorsement or
sponsorship of the religions in question and argue against
the recognition of such days and festivals by the state at all.
It is, however, difficult to reconcile this reaction with the
acknowledged role of the state as the neutral and impartial
organiser of religious life and, more particularly, the need to
ensure that religious groups have access to legal personality.
In the cases concerning registration of religious organisations, the Court repeatedly says that 'a refusal by the domestic authorities to grant legal-entity status to an association of individuals may amount to an interference with the
applicants' exercise of their right to freedom of association
.... Where the organisation of the religious community is
at issue, a refusal to recognise it also constitutes interference with the applicants' right to freedom of religion under
Article 9'.[3] Although this is, strictly speaking, functional in
its significance, it cannot be denied that in the granting of
such status to groups of religious believers and by permit-
ting them to function as legal entities in the public sphere
the state is according them a degree of recognition which
has a symbolic as well as practical relevance by recognising
them 'as' religious. This is not to say, of course, that those
groups of believers which, for whatever reason, might *not*
be accorded official recognition are not religious in nature
or that individual adherents are not free to enjoy their
freedom of religion or belief, since the Court has made it
abundantly clear that the state is not to make judgements
of this kind. However, through its regulatory activities the
state is involved – and cannot avoid being involved – in
decision-making which is symbolically significant.

Once seen from this perspective, a whole host of other
regulatory activities take on a similar significance, the most
obvious of which concern planning laws, which convert
what might be termed 'conceptual' symbolic visibility
into more 'tangible' symbolic visibility. One of the clear-
est manifestations of religion within a community are the
presence of religious structures. The freedom of religion or

---

3   *Church of Scientology Moscow v. Russia*, op.cit., para 81, 5 April
2007.

belief clearly encompasses the right to have and to maintain places of worship and their presence is a powerful marker within a community. It goes without saying that religious buildings are a symbolic presence in and of themselves and their distinctive architecture and adornment, as well as the activities which take place in and around them, again take on a symbolic meaning which is at once both 'conceptual' and 'tangible': the presence of a minaret or church tower dominating the skyline in a town or village is more than the mere physical display of a symbol but is a statement of a physical presence within the community, with the size and location of such buildings being similarly significant.

Many other examples could be given but enough has already been said to make the point that the state is intimately involved in many matters which are symbolically significant from a religious perspective. Two points need to be made which flow from this. First, since it is engaging with such issues on an ongoing basis from a variety of public law perspectives there is no reason for a state to shy away from regulating matters concerning religious symbols. When religious believers and organised religion enter the public arena their activities, in common with those of all other participants, are subject to the legislative and regulatory powers of the state (which are of course to be exercised in accordance with human rights law). Secondly, it shows that it cannot be seriously maintained that the duty of neutrality and impartiality means that religious symbolism is to be removed from the public space, generally understood. Article 9 itself makes it clear that the freedom of religion includes the freedom to manifest beliefs 'in public' and this, of necessity, requires that the state facilitates rather than frustrates this through its regulation of the public domain. The critical question is not so much whether there is a religious symbol, or a matter which is of religious symbolic significance, which is at sake: rather, it is the context in which it occurs which matters most.

This can be illustrated by looking at two contrasting cases. The first is *Buscarini v. San Marino* in which the applicant, who had been elected to Parliament, argued that his freedom of belief had been infringed by his being required to swear an oath of allegiance 'on the Holy Gospel'. The Court endorsed the view that 'it would be contradictory to make the exercise of a mandate intended to represent different views of society within Parliament subject to a

It is beyond doubt that an individual has the right to make a public declaration of their faith – but it is equally the case that the state may place restrictions on when, where and how – context is vital.

prior declaration of commitment to a particular set of beliefs'.[4] Clearly, a person swearing an oath underwritten by a religious pledge carries with it a high degree of symbolic meaning. This may be entirely appropriate when voluntarily undertaken by the person concerned in order to emphasise the seriousness of the commitment being undertaken *by them* in public settings. But is it completely inappropriate when it is a requirement of participation in democratic governance. The second is *Sofianopoulos v. Greece*, in which the applicants argued that they should be able to record their religious affiliation on their official Identity Cards if they wished to do so, in order that they be able to make their beliefs known publicly. In declaring the application inadmissible, the Court noted that it was for the state to determine what information was appropriate and said that 'the purpose of an identity card is not to bolster its bearer's religious feelings'.[5] Once again, it is beyond doubt that an individual has the right to make a public declaration of their faith – but it is equally the case that the state may place re-strictions on when, where and how. As both these examples show, context is vital.

(B)   What Is a 'Religious Symbol'?

Since determining what comprises a religious symbol is not a straightforward task, it might seem appropriate to seek some objective benchmarks. These, however, are difficult to come by.

(a)   'Objects of religious veneration'

In the *Otto-Preminger-Institut* case the Court spoke of 'ob-jects of religious veneration' and, as we have seen, provoca-tive portrayals of such objects by others may amount to a 'malicious violation of the spirit of tolerance'.[6] As a class of object receiving a specific and heightened form of protec-tion within the Convention system, it might be thought that some guidance as to what might fall within the category

---

4   *Buscarini and others v. San Marino* [GC], no 24645/94, para 39, ECHR 1999-I.

5   *Sofianopoulos and Others v. Greece (dec.)*, nos. 1988/02, 1997/02, 1977/02, p. 8, ECHR 2002-X.

6   *Otto-Preminger-Institut v. Austria*, op.cit., para 47.

of 'religious symbols' might be had by looking at what is meant by an 'object of religious veneration'? This, however, is problematic for a number of reasons.

It is possible to understand this term in a narrower or a broader fashion. The *Otto-Preminger-Insitut* case concerned a film, 'Das Liebeskonzil' which portrayed 'the God of the Jewish, the Christian and the Islamic religion as an apparently senile old man .... a degree of erotic tension between the Virgin Mary and the Devil [and] the adult Jesus Christ ... as a low grade mental defective'.[7] The film at the centre of the subsequent *Wingrove* case, 'Visions of Ecstasy' portrayed 'a female character astride the recumbent body of the crucified Christ engaged in an act of an overtly sexual nature' and national authorities considered the film to be primarily pornographic in nature, with 'no attempt ... to explore the meaning of the imagery beyond engaging the viewer in a "voyeuristic erotic experience"'.[8] The 'objects of religious veneration' at issue in both of these cases might perhaps have been better described as 'figures of religious devotion', since the focus was on the personage of the deity and others to whom religious homage was paid. It is, therefore, possible to understand these cases in a narrow fashion in which only portrayals of such figures themselves would be addressed.

A broader view would be to see an 'object of religious veneration' including all those things which form an element in the religious life of a believer and contribute to the exercise of the freedom to manifest their religion or belief in worship, teaching, practice and observance. This might embrace items as diverse as forms of clothing, utensils, written materials, pictures, buildings and a whole host of additional items impossible to specify. For example, the early case of *X and the Church of Scientology* v. *Sweden* concerned an injunction that had been awarded against the applicants prohibiting them from advertising the sale of an 'E Meter', described a 'A religious artefact used to measure the state of the electrical characteristics of the "static field" surrounding the body and believed to reflect or indicate whether or not the confessing person has been relieved of the spiritual impediment of their sins.' The Commission considered the advertisement to be more commercial than

---

7   *Ibid*, para 22.

8   *Wingrove v. the United Kingdom*, op.cit., para 61.

religious in nature, but the religious nature of the artefact was not contested.[9] Clearly, the E-meter was not an object of religious veneration although it was seen as playing a role in the religious life of the believer.

The concept of 'objects of religious veneration', then, would seem to be broader than the narrowly focussed idea of the 'deity' and narrower than the broad-based notion of those objects which are connected with the act of religious observance. It is not possible, however, to define this term of art with any greater precision. Therefore, whilst this concept does offer a 'benchmark' against which to assess whether something is a religious symbol – since objects of religious veneration would be considered as religious symbols – and whilst symbols of this nature attract an assured level of protection under the Convention system, it is unhelpful to seek to understand what is to be taken to be a religious symbol solely by reference to it. Moreover, the idea of a 'symbol' is broader than that of an 'object of veneration' since it may include those things which, whilst not themselves objects of veneration, are representations of objects of veneration. An obvious example would be a crucifix or an icon. Of course, it is possible for representations of objects of veneration to become objects of veneration, thus making any classificatory approach impossible.

(b) Religious symbols: An objective or subjective matter?

The impossibility of determining *a priori* what is to be taken as a religious symbol for all Convention purposes is underscored by combination of the private dimension of the freedom of religion or belief and the principle of neutrality and impartiality. The Court has said on numerous occasions that 'the freedom of religion ... excludes any discretion on the part of the state to determine whether religious beliefs or the means used to express such beliefs are legitimate'.[10] It would seem to follow from this that it is for the individual, rather than for the state or for the Court, to determine whether something is, for them, a religious symbol. It is difficult to see on what basis the state or the Court could deny the symbolic significance of something

---

9   *X and the Church of Scientology v. Sweden*, op.cit.
10   See, for example, *Moscow Branch of the Salvation Army v. Russia*, op.cit., para 92.

which had been identified as being of such significance to them by the person concerned.

However, it cannot be emphasised enough that simply because something is considered to be a religious symbol does not mean that there is a right for it to be publicly visible. Indeed, whether something is or is not a religious symbol has relatively little relevance in and of itself when the question at issue is whether that symbol may be displayed in some fashion *by the believer*. The reason is that this is subsumed within the more general question of what is to 'count' as a 'manifestation' of religion or belief. If, for example, the question concerns whether an individual may wear a prayer shawl, a cross, a turban or a headscarf in a public setting, it does not matter whether those items are or are not religious symbols: the relevant question is whether that person is manifesting their religion or belief by the wearing or the displaying of it. This is clear from those cases which have dealt with issues concerning religiously-inspired clothing. For example, in the case of the *Moscow Branch of the Salvation Army v. Russia* the Court accepted that 'It is indisputable that for members .... wearing uniforms were particular ways of ... manifesting The Salvation Army's religious beliefs'[11] and in *Leyla Şahin v. Turkey* the Grand Chamber endorsed the view of the Chamber that:[12]

> 'The applicant said that, by wearing the headscarf, she was obeying a religious precept and thereby manifesting her desire to comply strictly with the duties imposed by the Islamic faith. Accordingly, her decision to wear the headscarf may be regarded as motivated or inspired by a religion or belief and, without deciding whether such decisions are in every case taken to fulfil a religious duty, the Court proceeds on the assumption that the regulations in issue, which placed restrictions of place and manner on the right to wear the Islamic headscarf in universities, constituted an interference with the applicant's right to manifest her religion.'

Once again, the Court approached the matter on the basis of the wearing of the headscarf being a 'manifestation' of religion or belief. Indeed, it might be noted in passing that the Court chose not to draw on the distinction drawn in the *Arrowsmith* case between acts which are motivated by

it is for the individual, rather than for the state or for the Court, to determine whether something is, for them, a religious symbol. But simply because something is considered to be a religious symbol does not mean that there is a right for it to be publicly visible.

---

11   *Idem.*

12   *Leyla Şahin v. Turkey* [GC], op.cit., para 78.

religion or belief but which fall short of being a manifestation of religion or belief. Rather, it proceeded on the basis that the refusal to allow the applicant to wear attire which she considered to be warranted by her religious beliefs was sufficient to amount to an interference with the freedom to manifest those beliefs. It was irrelevant as far as the Court was concerned whether others of her religious persuasion took a similar view. It was also irrelevant whether the headscarf was or was not a 'religious symbol' at this point in the judgment. What mattered was whether it was a *bona fide* manifestation of her religious beliefs. It might be concluded that, from the point of view of the persons wishing to display a religious symbol, what matters is that they are manifesting their beliefs, not that they are manifesting them through the display of a religious symbol.

(c)   *The role of the third party*

Perhaps surprisingly, the real significance of something being a religious symbol lies in the response of others to that symbol. There are two dimensions to this. We have already seen how that sub-set of symbols which comprise objects of religious veneration may be protected from being the subject of 'provocative portrayals' since such portrayals may amount to a 'malicious violation of the spirit of tolerance'. When seen from this perspective, it becomes clearer why there is a tendency to focus on a narrower rather than a broader approach to what is to be considered as an 'object of religious veneration'. What is necessary for the purposes of fostering pluralism and tolerance is that respect be shown to the religion or belief in question, rather than that respect be shown to those things which particular individuals might consider to be invested with personal religious significance. A related situation occurs when non-believers use signs or items in a fashion which may cause offence to believers for whom they have a religious significance. For example, not every turban or headscarf, cross, knife or bracelet has a religious significance for the wearer. Such objects might, however, have a religious significance for someone else who might consider their use or display by non-believers to be offensive. Although there is no interference with the manifestation of religion or belief in such situations there may be a lack of respect sufficient to warrant some form of response by the state, particularly if there is a lack of 'parity' in the relationship. Just as in *Larrisis* v.

Greece,[13] discussed above, the Court decided that the state was entitled to take action to prevent officers in the Greek airforce from proselytising to junior airmen, so would the state be entitled to take action if a person in a position of power or dominance used that position to abuse or besmirch the religious symbols of another. In such situations, the state is not 'protecting' the religion from criticism but it is fulfilling its role as the neutral and impartial organiser of religious life by taking steps to ensure that there is a 'level playing field'.

A second dimension concerns the impact which a symbol has on others who are not believers. In many ways this raises more difficult questions since it might result in the same symbol being invested with a different symbolic meaning by different observers, thus complicating the balancing of the conflicting rights which needs to be undertaken. For example, in the *Şahin* case it was taken as read that the wearing of the Islamic headscarf was of religious significance to the applicant and a means through which she manifested her religious beliefs. It was also accepted that 'there are extremist political movements in Turkey which seek to impose on society as a whole their religious symbols and conception of a society founded on religious precepts.'[14] The Court also recalled that in the *Refah Partisi* case it had noted that 'in the past political movements based on religious fundamentalism have been able to seize political power in certain states and have had the opportunity to set up the model of society which they had in mind. It considers that, in accordance with the Convention's provisions, each Contracting state may oppose such political movements in the light of its historical experience.'[15] Whether the applicant was or was not involved in such a political movement was of secondary importance to the outcome of the case. What for the applicant might be a matter of personal piety might have a high degree of political significance for others and, irrespective of whether that political implication is justified or not, this alone might require that the state respond to the emergent situation in order to resolve any resulting tensions. The example of re-routing religious processions in areas of inter-religious hostility might provide an example of such a

13   *Larissis and others v. Greece*, judgment of 24 February 1998, *Reports of Judgments and Decisions*, 1998-I.

14   *Leyla Şahin v. Turkey* [GC], op.cit., para 115.

15   *Ibid.*, para 124.

situation. The key point is that what justifies the response of the state to the display of religious affiliation is not so much that display in itself, but the responses to that display in that particular context *by others*.

> What justifies the response of the state to the display of religious affiliation is not so much that display in itself, but the responses to that display in that particular context by others.

There are, then, some symbols which are so closely associated with a particular form of religion or belief that any form of display of them might reasonably be associated with the faith in question – the Hijab and a Crucifix might immediately be thought of – although on close examination of the facts it might turn out that they were not being displayed for religious reasons at all. Likewise there are many markers of religious affiliation which might be invested with a degree of religious symbolism by non-believers irrespective of whether the bearer considers them to be a 'religious symbol'. In all cases, the assessments may be context driven. In short, it is difficult to offer any categoric answers to the abstract question of 'what is a religious symbol' as the answer may change from time to time and vary from place to place. In many – perhaps in most – cases it will not be a difficult question to answer, but the foregoing discussion has tried to emphasise the need to think beyond the question of 'what is a religious symbol' and consider the larger question of 'what is understood to be religiously symbolic' in a given situation. This makes the matter more contextually rooted and, as will be seen in the final section of this Manual, it is the context which drives the determination of when it is legitimate to restrict the wearing of a religious symbol.

(C) 'Wearing' Symbols and the Scope of the Manual

If one were to take the title of this Manual literally, it would only be concerned with a very small subset of instances in which the visibility of religious symbols requires consideration from a Convention perspective – occasions on which religious symbols were being 'worn'. The previous section has drawn attention to the need to ensure that the expression 'religious symbol' is approached and understood in context and it is equally important to ensure that the approach taken to the 'wearing' of religious symbols is similarly congruent with the more general policies regarding religious symbolism in the public arena. Because of this, it is probably unwise as well as unnecessary to dwell at length on what is meant by 'wearing' a religious symbol. It does, however, need to be stressed that the linkage between 'wearing' and 'symbols' for the purposes of this Manual must not influence an understanding of what a religious symbol is: many things which are religiously symbolic are not necessarily capable of being described as being religious symbols and it would be doubly unfortunately if emphasis was placed upon the 'wearing' of 'symbols' rather than placing this debate within the broader context of regulating matters of religious symbolic significance.

For example, it might be possible to prevent teachers and school children from wearing religious clothing (as will be discussed in the final section of this Manual). However, if the school itself is run by a religious body or along confessional lines, then it may be exuding an ethos which is equally, if not more, significant in terms of the practical impact it may have on the children, irrespective of whether teachers or pupils wear religious symbols or not. Likewise, the educational curriculum in a school may be such as to lend a degree of emphasis to a particular form of belief. We have already seen how Article 2 of the First Protocol to the Convention requires that the state respects the rights of parents to have their children educated in accordance with their religious or philosophical convictions. In the case of *Zengin v. Turkey*, the Court noted that:

> 'the syllabus for teaching in primary schools and the first cycle of secondary school, and all of the textbooks drawn up in accordance with the Ministry of Education's decision no. 373 of 19 September 2000, give greater priority to knowledge of Islam than they do to that of other religions and philosophies. In the Court's view, this itself cannot be viewed as a departure from the principles of pluralism and objectivity which would amount to indoctrination ... having regard to the fact that, notwithstanding the state's secular nature, Islam is the majority religion practised in Turkey'.[16]

The Court did in fact conclude that the nature of the syllabus strayed beyond the bounds of what was legitimate since as it appeared to include elements of doctrinal instruction adequate and effective opt-out mechanisms needed to be in place which, on the facts of the case, were lacking. However, what needs to be stressed for current purposes

---

16   *Hasan and Eylem Zengin v. Turkey*, no. 1448/04, para 63, ECHR 2007.

is the simple point that it would be strange to be overly concerned with the wearing of religious symbols by pupils or teachers in a classroom setting if the curriculum which is being delivered within that classroom can legitimately give priority to a dominant faith tradition provided appropriate opt-outs are in place.

The focus on the 'wearing' of a religious symbol has the capacity to distort our understanding of what a religious symbol actually is, and arguably extend its scope further than is necessary. As has been seen, the Court has accepted without hesitation the claim that wearing a headscarf may be a manifestation of Islamic belief. It is certainly the case that for many of other faiths and of none the wearing of a headscarf is understood to be religiously significant for Muslims. It is also the case that wearing the headscarf may be symbolically significant in numerous ways: for the wearer, it may be an assertion of their religious identity; to the observer, it may be a means of recognition; to society, it may be an indicator of the existence of religious pluralism and tolerance. Others may see the practice as symbolising more negative features. But it must be noted that a headscarf (like many other indicia) may fulfil all of these roles simultaneously but still not necessarily be a 'religious symbol'. What converts it into a symbol is the nature of the significance with which it is invested and, as we have seen, this may be context driven. There is a danger in equating all those things which people might wear, or the manner in which they choose to present themselves, as religious symbols rather than as forms of manifestation of religion or belief: doing so may result in their becoming invested with a greater significance than is appropriate, making it at the same time both more desirable and yet more difficult to place limitations on them.

It should also be recalled that insofar as the Manual is focussing on the visibility of religious symbolism in the public arena, the question of whether or not a religious symbol is being 'worn' may be a wholly artificial distinction. For example, it follows from previous discussion that there is little sense in prohibiting a judge from wearing religious insignia if their judicial function is carried out against the trappings of religiosity (e.g. in the nature of oaths to be sworn, etc), unless there is evidence to suggest that the personal views of the judge may be unduly influenced by their beliefs.[17] Likewise, if crosses may be physically present in classrooms, it is more difficult to see why those working in them should be prohibited from wearing them. Of course, it may well be that both ought to be prohibited but the point is that the broader context needs to be taken into account when determining the matter.

The focus on wearing symbols can also result in some rather bizarre outcomes. For example, a girl with an Islamic headscarf or a boy with a skull-cup might reasonably be described as 'wearing' a symbol of their religious commitment. Likewise with a piece of jewellery. It is less obvious that a male Sikh carrying a kirpan in his belt is 'wearing' as opposed to 'carrying' a symbol of his religiosity. It is probable that one 'wears' a beard, though one does not generally 'wear' one's hair. It is, however, difficult to see the reason for differentiating facial from non-facial hair growth. Whilst it might reasonably be claimed that some Rastafarians, Jews and Sikhs (*inter alia*) 'wear' their hair in a particular fashion for religiously motivated reasons, it strains the normal use of language somewhat to say that those who 'shave' their heads are 'wearing' a bald head. Advancing the argument in this fashion again raises the question of whether a shaved head really is properly characterised as a 'religious symbol' and, if it is it not, then it is not clear why objects which cover the head or body are a religious symbol *per se*, as opposed to a mark of a person's religious devotion which may be invested with a symbolic significance by others. If a further example be needed, a number of religious traditions call for male circumcision. It can hardly be said that one 'wears' a circumcised penis, nor can a circumcised penis be fairly described as a religious symbol; yet for believers the practice is it undoubtedly a manifestation of belief (though admittedly rarely – legally – in public).[18]

Since it has chosen to focus on whether something is or is not a manifestation of religion or belief rather than on

---

17 See, for example, *Kalaç v. Turkey*, op.cit, paras 25 and where the Court agreed with the Government that 'by taking and carrying out instructions from the leaders of the sect Group Captain Kalaç had breached military discipline'.

18 Changing rooms in publicly-run schools and sports facilities provide an example, however. The question of what is meant by a 'public' area will be considered further below.

the question of whether something is or is not a religious symbol, the European Court has not yet allowed itself to be confused by these difficulties. There have, however, been examples of such confusion within domestic jurisdictions. For example, the case of *Playfoot* v. *Governing Body of Millais School*[19] centred on the desire of a young teenage Christian girl to wear a silver ring at school 'as a symbol of her commitment to celibacy before marriage' and which she considered to be a sign of her beliefs as a Christian. Wearing rings was contrary to the School's uniform policy which did not permit jewellery to be worn. The domestic Court, following the approach in *Arrowsmith* v. *the United Kingdom*,[20] took the view that whilst the wearing of the ring was motivated by her beliefs, it was not a manifestation of them and so Article 9 was not engaged. It seems, however, that the Court reached this conclusion because it thought there was no evidence that her beliefs as a Christian 'required' her to wear the ring, which was sufficient to distinguish it from cases in which Sikh girls had been permitted to wear bracelets and Muslim and Plymouth Brethren girls had been permitted to wear headscarves, and it endorsed the view that the ring was not a 'Christian symbol'. This seems to equate the manifestation of belief with the wearing of a symbol, which, for reasons already given, is questionable. Moreover, when considering the issue of the proportionality of the restriction the domestic Court noted that there were other options open to her since she could 'attach her rings, or a keyring or other visible sign, to her bag'.[21]

This suggests that the Court was really focussing on the very narrow question of whether an exception should be made to the policy of not allowing girls to wear jewellery and it set a very high threshold: only in those instances in which jewellery (or clothing) is required to be worn as a matter of religious obligation might an exception be necessary. Interestingly, and crucially, there was no difficulty about displaying the ring in other ways – such as on her bag – and so the restriction was more to do with the means of display rather than the fact of display. The symbolic significance of a ring worn on a finger is potentially much greater than that of a ring displayed on a bag and it is difficult to

---

19 *Playfoot* v. *Governing Body of Millais School,* [2007] EWHC 1698 (Admin).

20 *Arrowsmith* v. *UK, op.cit.*

21 *Playfoot* v. *Governing Body of Millais School, op.cit.,* para 38 (iii).

see why wearing a ring is more problematic than displaying a ring, save for the existence of the policy at issue.

Either way, the justification for the policy and the restriction has little relevance to the question of whether or not the display of such a ring is religiously motivated, religiously symbolic or, indeed, whether the ring is or is not a religious symbol. Indeed, seen in this light, the question of whether the ring was or was not a religious symbol (as opposed to a practice motivated by, reflective of, or even required by ones beliefs) is, strictly speaking, irrelevant. This is not to say that there are not religious symbols which may be worn, – the Christian cross being a clear example and one to which we will return – but to focus the debate upon questions of whether something is or is not a religious symbol a requirement of religious observance and then to juxtapose this upon the question of its being worn, is to run the risk of missing the broader and more significant issue which is at stake. That broader, underlying question concerns the visibility of religion within the public sphere and how to reconcile the need to permit believers to enjoy the freedom to manifest their religion or belief in public whilst respecting the rights and freedoms of others in a fashion which is respectful of the rights of all concerned, is neutral and impartial and fosters a climate of pluralism and tolerance. The key to determining whether a restriction is or is not justified turns less on whether something is or is not a religious symbol or on whether it is or is not being worn (though this is not to say these are unimportant issues) than on the application of these wider desiderata to the specifics of a particular situation within the public realm. The final part of this section will, then, look at this third definitional issue that flows from the focus on this Manual, the 'public area'.

> The underlying question concerns the visibility of religion within the public sphere and how to reconcile the need to permit believers to enjoy the freedom to manifest their religion or belief in public whilst respecting the rights and freedoms of others in a fashion which fosters a climate of pluralism and tolerance.

(D) What is a 'Public Area'?

The title of this Manual focusses attention on the wearing of religious symbols in 'public areas'. This is not a 'term of art' and there is no generally agreed understanding of what is meant by 'public area' within the European Convention system. As with the other definitional issues already considered, a number of different approaches are possible.

(a) The pitfalls of a literalist approach

One approach would be to take the words 'public area' literally and limit the scope of the Manual to those places which are public in the sense of being open and accessible to all, such as streets, parks, etc. If combined with a narrow view of what was meant by a 'religious symbol' and by the term 'wearing', so narrow an approach would empty the subject of much of its interest and address very few practical issues. Should a broader view be taken of what comprises a 'religious symbol', so as to include those things which are a marker of religious affiliation rather than 'symbols' *per se*, this would permit situations in which certain forms of religious dress are prohibited from being seen in public at all to be included within its scope. However, since it is only in the most exceptional circumstances that such a complete prohibition could be justifiable under Article 9(2) this would also be too narrow an approach to make a Manual worthwhile.

Taking an overly broad approach to these terms is, however, equally problematic and over-extends the scope of the Manual. If, for example, a broad approach was taken to what comprises a religious symbol which focussed on the idea of visibility, or display, rather than on the 'wearing' of a religious symbol, then taking a similarly broad approach to what is to be understood as a 'public area' – such as, for example, any situation in which a religious symbol might be seen by a member of the public – the result would be a situation in which the public visibility of anything which was representational of religion or belief would fall within its scope. Adopting such a broad-ranging approach produces very real problems. Although any restrictions on the public visibility of religion would still need to be justified in terms of Article 9(2), it would have the practical effect of requiring religious believers and religious bodies to account for their presence in the community in a fashion which fails to respect the basic principles regarding the freedom of religion or belief set out in the *Kokkinakis* case,[22] which emphasises the significance of religion and religious diversity as an essential component of a flourishing plural democratic society rather than as something which needs to be explained and justified. It would also mean that the Manual would have to address a whole host of additional questions,

---

22   *Kokkinakis v. Greece*, op.cit.

such as issues concerning planning law and the location and design of religious buildings, which might fairly be considered as lying well beyond its scope.

(b) *An alternative approach: the 'public domain'*

It is, then, necessary to steer a path between these two extremes. Moreover, both of these approaches tend to emphasise the physical dimension of the expression 'public area' rather than its more conceptual dimension. It seems to be more appropriate to focus on the idea of the 'public' rather than on the idea of the 'area' or 'place' when dealing with this issue. This receives powerful support from the *Otto-Preminger-Institut* case which, as we have seen, concerned the legitimacy of the seizure and destruction of a film which was considered to be offensive in its disrespect for objects of religious veneration. The film was to have been shown in a private cinema, accessible to the public only on a fee-paying basis and this, the applicant argued, was sufficient to prevent unwarranted offence. The Court disagreed, saying that

> 'although access to the cinema to see the film was subject to payment of an admission fee and an age limit, the film was widely advertised. There was sufficient public knowledge of the subject matter and basic contents of the film to give a clear indication of its nature; for this reason, the proposed screening of the film must be considered to have been an expression sufficiently 'public' to cause offence'.[23]

This suggests that what is to be taken as comprising the 'public' domain should be approached in a purposive rather than a literalist fashion. Therefore, this Manual focuses not so much the wearing of religious symbols in public or in public places but on the presence of religious symbolism in what might be called the 'public arena' or, more generally, in 'public life'; that is, in the areas of public engagement which fall to be conducted or regulated by the state.

This approach is reflected in the case-law of the Court. The Court emphasises that the role of the state is to be the 'neutral and impartial organiser' of the exercise of various religions, beliefs and faiths, this being 'conducive to public

This Manual focusses on the presence of religious symbolism in the areas of public engagement which fall to be conducted or regulated by the state.

---

23   *Otto-Preminger Institut v. Austria*, op.cit., para 54.

order, religious harmony and tolerance in a democratic society'.[24] According to Article 9 itself, the freedom of religion or belief may be manifested 'in public or in private' and restricted only in pursuit of the legitimate aims of preserving certain public goods, including the rights and freedoms of others. None of this has any direct connection with the nature of the 'place' as being a public area in a literal sense of the word. Rather, they are concerned with the manner in which states respond to situations in which the presence of religious symbols, or of things which are considered to be symbolic of religion, give rise to questions. For example, *Leyla Şahin v. Turkey* concerned a prohibition on the wearing of headscarves and of beards to lectures, courses or tutorials at Istanbul University based on a circular issued by the University's Vice-Chancellor in the light of a ruling of the Constitutional Court. Students with beards or who wore headscarves to lectures or tutorials were required to leave and were not to be registered as students. Only registered students were entitled to attend lectures or tutorials. The Court noted that Universities were 'public-law bodies by virtue of Article 130 of the Constitution, they enjoy a degree of autonomy, subject to state control, that is reflected in the fact that they are run by management organs .... with delegated statutory powers'.[25] Nevertheless, they were certainly not 'public' in the sense of being generally accessible: Universities were 'public' by virtue of the manner in which they were constituted and because of the nature of the function – public education – which they fulfilled.

A similar point can be made in respect of cases in which restrictions have been placed on those working for the state. Public servants may reasonably be expected to be subject to such regulations even when their work does not bring them into contact with 'the public' or is undertaken in a 'public setting': it is the public nature of their employment which is the starting point for there being a restriction, the context or nature of that employment then being a factor which might influence a decision on whether a restriction is or is not justified. It is clear that the public nature of employment is not sufficient to justify a restriction *per se*. Indeed, cases such as *Knudsen v. Norway*[26] remind us that in some

---

24   *Refah Partisi (the Welfare Party) and* Others *v. Turkey* [GC], op.cit., para 91.

25   *Leyla Şahin v. Turkey* [GC], op.cit., para 54.

26   *Knudsen v. Norway,* op.cit.

countries ministers of religion are themselves state employees, or are employed by the state to fulfil public functions in a religious capacity. Moreover, in many countries both the state itself and other public bodies employ members of religious communities to work in a religious capacity, such as in hospitals and the armed forces. Given the nature of their employment it would be bizarre if such employees were prohibited from wearing religious symbols whilst fulfilling their duties as public servants as this would contradict the very reason for their employment. This, then reinforces the need to assess each situation carefully on its particular facts and in the light of the overall context.

(c)   Positive obligations and the public domain

A further issue arises from the 'positive' dimension of the obligations upon the state. On a general level, the Court has said that:

> 'In determining the scope of a state's positive obligations, regard must be had to the fair balance that has to be struck between the general interest and the interest of the individual, the diversity of situations obtaining in Contracting states and the choices which must be made in terms of priorities and resources. Nor must these obligations be interpreted in such a way as to impose an impossible or disproportionate burden.'[27]

It is important to bear this in mind when considering what might be required of a state in this regard. Nevertheless, as has been seen the Court has made it clear that whilst states must not intrude into the '*forum internum*' of the individual, or into the internal life of a religious or belief community, they are under a duty to ensure that there is a 'level playing field' in the contestation of ideas between believers and also between believers and non-believers. The relevant question is whether this only applies in the 'public' sphere or whether it also extends to the 'private'.

It should also be recalled that the Court has said that it is not the role of the state to remove causes of tension within divided communities, and although this was said in the

It is the role of the state to take steps to ensure that there is a degree of mutual respect between competing groups and in the presentation of different ideas and opinions.

---

27   *Ilaşcu and others* v. *Moldova and Russia* [GC], no 48787/99, para 332, ECHR 2004-VII.

context of state involvement in the resolution of leadership struggles within religious organisations, this may fairly be taken as also applying to divided political communities; divided in the sense of being plural in their composition and offering different conceptions of life, in accordance with democratic principles. However, we have also seen that it is the role of the state to take steps to ensure that there is a degree of mutual respect between competing groups and in the presentation of different ideas and opinions. This, then, may not only legitimate state activism but may mandate it in cases where there is a lack of toleration and or respect. In short, there are clearly instances in which the state might not only choose to involve itself but may be in breach of its convention obligations if it does not take purposive action, as is seen by the case of *97 Members of the Gldani Congregation v. Georgia*,[28] discussed previously.

(d)   The difficulty of distinguishing the 'public' from the 'private' domain

The *Gldani* case is important for another reason. In the earlier case of *Kuznetsov v. Russia*[29] the state was held responsible for the actions of its agents who had acted in a private capacity when breaking up a service of worship. The *Gldani* case takes this further since the state was held responsible for its failure to prevent acts of violence meted out by one group of believers upon another group of believers, rather than because of any direct action taken by the state. The Court said that, 'through their inactivity, the relevant authorities failed in their duty to take the necessary measures to ensure that the group of Orthodox extremists led by Father Basil tolerated the existence of the applicants' religious community and enabled them to exercise freely their rights to freedom of religion'.[30] Thus the state was considered responsible for ensuring that private persons show respect and tolerance in matters of religion or belief in what might be considered private as well as in public settings, though the general caveats concerning the extent of that duty set

---

28   *Case of 97 Members of the Gldani Congregation of Jehovah's Witnesses and Others v. Georgia*, op.cit., para 134.

29   *Kuznetsov v. Russia*, op.cit.

30   *Case of 97 Members of the Gldani Congregation of Jehovah's Witnesses and Others v. Georgia*, ibid.

out in *Ilascu and others* v. *Moldova and Russia* and quoted above moderate the practical implications of this.

At one level, this is not surprising since a very clear breach of public order was involved in the *Gldani* case, and a very clear breach of the freedom to worship in the *Kznestov* case and it would be more remarkable if the state had not been found responsible under such circumstances. But the point of this for current purposes is that they again demonstrate that there is no very clear dividing line to be drawn between the 'public' and the 'private' space: what matters is the degree of interference with a convention right within the overall context of the Convention system. It is the failure to secure the convention right, as understood and interpreted by the jurisprudence of the Court, which is the relevant factor and the scope of the 'public sphere', or the 'public area' is ultimately bound up with that question. The development of 'positive obligations' and the duty to ensure toleration may carry this a long way into what generally might be thought to be the 'private' arena.[31]

Does this mean that the state might even be entitled to restrict the wearing or display of religious symbols in what might be considered to be private settings, such as meeting rooms belonging to religious of belief societies, or even in private homes? The short answer is yes, if that restriction is justified within the Convention system: the nature of the 'place' may affect the balancing act to be undertaken and make the restriction more difficult to justify but it does not exclude the possibility. There will, of course, be a very high threshold. In the case of *Laskey, Jaggard and Brown v. the United Kingdom*[32] the Court was faced with the question of whether the state might criminalise sadomasochistic

---

31   Although not made explicit at the time, this is apparent from the very earliest cases concerning the scope of Article 9 and the obligation to show 'respect' for objects of religious veneration. For example, this is evident from the *Otto-Preminger-Institut* case, quoted above, and also from the subsequent case of *Wingrove v. the United Kingdom*, op.cit., para 63 where the Court rejected the view that the limited distribution of a film in video form through a controlled network reduced the risk of its causing offence, saying that 'it is in the nature of video works that … they can in practice be copied, lent, rented sold and viewed in different homes thereby easily escaping any form of control by the authorities'.

32   *Laskey, Jaggard and Brown v. the United Kingdom*, judgment of 19 February 1997, *Reports of Judgments and Decisions* 1997-I.

sexual practices undertaken by consenting adults in private. It concluded that it was, largely on the grounds that the state was entitled to take steps to prevent the infliction of physical harm. In cases not involving such harm it has still taken the view that it is only where there is an emergent common European consensus that it might intervene in order to prevent the prohibition of private activities which the state considers to be contrary to the broader public interest. Thus in *Dudgeon* v. *the UK* the Court, commenting on the continued criminalisation of consensual homosexual conduct in Northern Ireland, said that 'Although members of the public who regard homosexuality as immoral may be shocked, offended or disturbed by the commission by others of private homosexual act, this cannot on its own warrant the application of penal sanctions when it is consenting adults alone who are involved'.[33]

We have already seen that the Court does not consider there to be a common European consensus regarding the place of religion or belief in public life. What it does recognise is that states may take account of the nature of their political structures and their sense of national identity and that judgments in cases such as *Refah Partisi v. Turkey* point to the limits of religious influence in the political life of the community. Where it is clearly established on the facts that the display of religious symbols even in a purely private setting is indicative of beliefs and activities which threaten the rights and freedoms of others, then the possibility of their being prohibited cannot be entirely excluded. In the case of *Laskey, Jaggard and Brown v. the United Kingdom* the European Court agreed with the domestic court that 'in deciding whether or not to prosecute, the state authorities were entitled to have regard not only to the actual seriousness of the harm caused – which as noted above was considered to be significant – but also .... to the potential for harm inherent in the acts in question'.[34]

All of this combines to suggest that where the knowledge of the use of religious symbolism even within a private setting is such as to pose a genuine threat to the integrity of the democratic structures or to public morals, health or order, or to the rights and freedoms of others, then the state may,

---

33   *Dudgeon v. the United Kingdom,* judgment of 22 October 1981, Series A no. 45, para 60.

34   *Laskey, Jaggard and Brown v. the United Kingdom,* op.cit., para 46.

subject to rigorous European supervision, take proportionate measures to restrict their use. It also combines to reinforce the point that not only is the idea of a public 'area' too limited a context within which to understand the legitimacy of restraints upon the utilisation of religious symbolism but that the entire notion of the public/private divide is exceedingly porous when the wearing of religious symbols is at issue.

(E) Conclusion

The previous subsections have explored the key definitional issues that emerge from the title of this Manual in the light of the jurisprudence of the Court relating to the freedom of religion or belief, these being what are 'religious symbols' and what is meant by the expressions 'wearing' and the 'public area'. It has been seen that none of these terms have been defined in a clear fashion by the Court and they can all be interpreted in a variety of different ways. It is suggested that the most appropriate way forward is to consider these terms in a purposive fashion, which itself reflects the idea that the Convention is not static but is a 'living instrument'. A purposive approach to these terms – and, therefore, to the scope of the Manual as a whole – allows for the inter-dependencies between these terms to be recognised and allows for a holistic approach to be taken. Rather than consider whether the definitional requirements are met in any given situation, it is more appropriate to step back and to see if that situation as a whole is one which raises questions concerning the exercise of the freedom of religion which can best be addressed through considering the issue of the display of religious symbolism. This will vary from case to case, and reinforces the idea that resolution requires a contextual assessment. This contextual assessment takes place when the Court is called on to consider the legitimacy of any restriction placed upon the enjoyment of the freedom of religion or belief and it is to be informed by the principles identified and outlined earlier in this Manual, notably those of neutrality and impartiality, respect and the positive duty to foster pluralism and tolerance.

> This manual suggests taking a purposive approach to the notion of "wearing religious symbols in public areas" which requires making a contextual assessment.

#VII The Wearing of Religious Symbols: The practical Application of the Principles Identified

The conclusions reached in the previous section give some guidance as to how the jurisprudence of the court is to be understood and how cases in which applicants argue that their freedom to manifest their religion or belief has been trenched upon as a result of their being unable to display or wear items of symbolic significance to them may be resolved by the Court. The previous section also indicated the potential breadth of the topic and emphasised that it is not wise to make any *a priori* assumptions regarding the meaning of the key terms and issues upon which this Manual focusses. Although these are important conclusions, it must be acknowledged that they do not offer as much practical assistance to domestic policy makers as they might wish to be given. Domestic policy makers are likely to want specific guidance on the extent to which they are able to regulate the wearing of religious symbols either in general or in particular contexts, rather than an understanding of how the Court is likely to determine whether their decisions are compliant with the Convention and the principles and approaches it will draw on whilst doing so. Moreover, for all its possible ambiguities and extensions, there remains a very clear core to the question which involves items of clothing or religiously significant objects which mark out a person as being an adherent of a particular form of religion or belief system. The purpose of the final sections of this Manual is to offer such guidance, based on examples provided by the case-law of the European Court of Human Rights.

It needs to be stressed at the outset that this cannot be taken as offering 'definitive' guidance in relation to any particular heading since, in the final analysis, what is or is not appropriate will be context driven. The Court has made it clear that the state enjoys a broad margin of appreciation in determining how to give effect to its responsibilities as the neutral and impartial organiser of religious life whilst ensuring the fullest possible enjoyment of the freedom of religion or belief that is consistent with respect for the rights and freedoms of others. Moreover, conceptions of the proper balance to be struck have changed over time, and will continue to do so. The Court has itself recognised this, summing up the situation as follows:

> '... the meaning or impact of the public expression of a religious belief will differ according to time and context. Rules in this sphere will consequently vary from one country to another according to national traditions and the requirements imposed by the need to protect the rights and freedoms of others and to maintain public order'.[1]

It follows from this not only that the approaches adopted in some earlier cases may be less pertinent today but that even contemporary approaches may not necessarily be relevant in other states and in other contexts. However, bearing in mind these caveats, it is possible to identify categories of situations in which some common approaches are discernable and which either directly or by analogy offer some illustrative guidance to those setting domestic policy or implementing generic guidance in an operational setting.

(A)   The Basic Framework: A Brief Recapitulation

Since this section of the Manual may be read in its own right, it is prudent to begin by re-iterating the basic elements of the Article 9 framework relevant to this exercise. The first is that everyone has the right to manifest their religion or belief in teaching, worship, practice and observance. Although this does not expressly refer to the right to manifest religion or belief through the wearing or display of items of religious significance, the Court has been reluctant to dismiss claims on this basis. Thus in the case of the *Moscow Branch of the Salvation Army v. Russia* the Court accepted without question that the wearing of militaristic style uniforms was a manifestation of their beliefs.[2] In *Leyla Şahin v. Turkey* the Court proceeded on a slightly different basis, noting that the applicant claimed that, 'by wearing the headscarf, she was obeying a religious percept and thereby manifesting her desire to comply strictly with

---

1   *Leyla Şahin v. Turkey* [GC], op.cit., para 109.
2   *Moscow Branch of the Salvation Army v. Russia*, op.cit., para 92.

the duties imposed by the Islamic faith'. In its judgment the Court said that it 'proceeds on the assumption that the regulations in issue ..... constituted an interference with the applicant's right to manifest her religion,'[3] rather than accept that this was indeed the case and it took a similarly contingent view in its subsequent inadmissibility decision in the case of *Köse v. Turkey*.[4] However, the Court had tended to accept the view of the applicant when it comes to determining whether they are manifesting their beliefs in the manner of their clothing or apparel, irrespective of what others might consider to be the case. The Court also seems reluctant to conclude that applicants are merely 'motivated' by their beliefs when doing so since were it to do so this would mean that they would fall outside the scope of the protections offered by Article 9, though it has been willing to do so as regards other forms of behaviour which individuals might undertake on the basis of their beliefs.[5]

This approach is to be welcomed, as it recognises the autonomy of the individual and the essentially personal nature of the freedom of religion or belief. It also respects the overarching principle that it is not for the Court, or the state, to pass upon the legitimacy of any particular form of religion, or the manner in which a person seeks to manifest their faith. In short, if an individual believes that in wearing a particular form of clothing or by adorning themselves in a particular fashion they are following the dictates of their beliefs, then this self-assessment ought to be respected by others. Of course, this does not mean that it may not be subjected to restrictions and restraint, but if the freedom of religion embraces the right to wear religiously inspired clothing (and it clearly does) then it is not for others to say that an individual's personal perceptions of what their beliefs require of them is wrong.

The restrictions which may be placed upon the wearing of religiously inspired attire will usually need to be justified in accordance with Article 9(2), although there may be rare cases in which restrictions may also be justified in accordance with Articles 15 and 17. Since such instances are so unlikely no further consideration will be given to them

> If an individual believes that in wearing a particular form of clothing or by adorning themselves in a particular fashion they are following the dictates of their beliefs, then this self-assessment ought to be respected by others. Of course, this does not mean that it may not be subjected to restrictions and restraint.

3　*Leyla Şahin v. Turkey* [GC], op.cit., para 78.

4　*Köse and Others v. Turkey* (dec.), no. 26625/02, ECHR 2006-II.

5　See, for example, *Arrowsmith v. UK*, op.cit., and *Kosteski v. the former Yugoslav Republic of Macedonia*, op.cit.

here. When considering the legitimacy of restrictions, it is necessary to ensure that the restriction is prescribed by law and is 'necessary in a democratic society' to protect a range of public interests, notably the rights and freedoms of others. In some instances, questions may fall to be considered under other Articles of the Convention, such as Article 8(2) (private and family life), 10(2) (freedom of expression) or 11(2) (freedom of association) where the heads of restraint are slightly different and – more significantly – weight given to various factors the breadth of the margin of appreciation might differ. Nevertheless, focussing on the application of Article 9(2) is adequate for the purposes of gauging a general sense of what is permissible.

As has been seen, the Court accepts that states have a broad margin of appreciation which, in this context, has two dimensions. First, it means that since there is no common approach within Europe, 'where questions concerning the relationship between state and religions are at stake .... the role of the national decision-making body must be given special importance'.[6] This, then, permits the state to respond to such questions in a fashion which reflects its own particular understanding of that relationship, to the extent that this is compatible with the Convention as a whole. Secondly, having exercised this latitude in determining the overall context, it follows that '... the choice of the extent and form such regulations should take must inevitably be left up to a point to the state concerned, as it will depend on the domestic context concerned'.[7] It is at this point that the Court is to involve itself by determining whether the measures taken 'were justified in principle and proportionate'.[8] This brings us to the heart of the difficulties which this subject matter presents us with: the court says that in making this determination it 'must have regard to what is at stake'[9] and this is a question on which parties in dispute are likely to differ greatly. For example, in the case from which these citations are taken, *Leyla Şahin v. Turkey*, the applicant argued that she was simply seeking to follow the dictates of her religious beliefs and expressly declared that 'she was not seeking a legal recognition of a right for all

---

6   See, for example, *Leyla Şahin v. Turkey* [GC], op.cit., para 109.
7   Idem.
8   Ibid., para 110.
9   *Idem.*

women to wear the Islamic headscarf in all places'.[10] For the Court, however, what was at stake was 'the need to protect the rights and freedoms of others, to preserve public order and to secure civil peace and true religious pluralism'.[11] Given this assessment of what was at stake in the case, it is not difficult to see why the Court upheld the validity of the restriction. Determining what is at stake is, then, key to the task of assessing the proportionality of the measure in question and, of course, can only be determined on the facts of each case.

(B)   The Key Questions to Be Considered

When conducting this exercise decision-makers should be mindful of the basic principles and policies which have been identified and outlined earlier. When placing restrictions on the wearing of religious clothing and artefacts, the questions to be thougt about might include the following:

- is this restriction reflective of a general approach which is neutral and impartial as between all forms of religion or belief or does it seek to prioritise a particular conception of the good?
- is this restriction discriminatory in that it bears more directly or more harshly on the followers of one religion or belief than of another?
- is the restriction directly aimed at the protection of a 'legitimate interest' as set out in the Convention, and notably the protection of the rights and freedoms of others?
- is there a pressing reason why that interest needs to be protected?
- are there alternatives to the restriction which would secure the realisation of those interests and which would not involve a greater diminution of the freedom to manifest one's beliefs through the wearing of such religiously inspired clothing or artefacts?
- assuming there to be no other viable alternative approach, is the restriction limited to the minimum that is necessary to realise the specific legitimate aims identified?

---

10   *Ibid*, para 73.
11   *Ibid*, para 110.

– is the imposition of the restriction compatible with the principles of respect and or the need to foster tolerance and pluralism?

> The relevant question is not whether a restriction is 'reasonable' in all the circumstances of the case, but whether it is 'necessary'.

Above all else, it should be emphasised that the relevant question is not whether a restriction is 'reasonable' in all the circumstances of the case, but whether it is 'necessary' – which is a very different question and which sets a much higher threshold of legitimacy.

Should domestic policy and decision-makers address these questions when considering issues concerning restrictions upon the wearing of religious symbols, then it will be more likely that their decisions will be compliant with the Convention and be properly respectful of the freedom of religion whilst striking a fair balance between the competing interests at stake.

The Approach in Action: Areas of Practical Application

Having restated the guiding approach and the fundamental principles, and having distilled them into a number of key questions to be asked by policy and decision-makers in situations which arise from time to time, this final section will look at a number of key areas in which the core issue of religiously inspired clothing or attire has given rise to dispute, and at how this has been resolved. For all the reasons given previously, the primary focus will be on the jurisprudence of the European Court of Human Rights, though illustrations from other international fora and domestic jurisdictions will also be drawn on.

(A) Restrictions Flowing from Laws of General Application

The first category of restrictions is in some ways the most difficult to pin down, seemingly the least controversial but in practice may be the source of the most serious restrictions upon the wearing of religious symbols. Since it is something of a 'catch-all' it may seem odd to address it first but as the more specific areas considered in the following subsections are in some senses little more than specific applications of these more general restrictions it seems appropriate to deal with them in this order.

The law will often require that everyone acts or refrains from acting in a particular fashion. Such laws of general application may not raise any issues for some but may well do so for others and particularly for those who wish to act otherwise as a result of their religion or belief. These laws are not 'aimed at' or intended to address issues of religious clothing or symbols. There may have been no prior thought of their impact upon religious believers and it is laws such as these which often generate the 'classic' case of a violation of the Convention right, to which the solution may well lie in granting a special 'opt out' for a particular group of believers should this be considered justified.

(a)   The example of public safety

An excellent example of this approach concerns the compulsory wearing of crash helmets whilst riding motorbikes and hard hats whilst at work on building sites. Such regulations are intended to ensure that both workers in general and the general public benefit from appropriate health and safety legislation. In an early case involving the United Kingdom a Sikh, whose beliefs required him to wear a turban, had been convicted for offences under the Road Traffic Acts for failing to wear a crash-helmet. The Commission decided that although there had been an interference with his freedom of religion, this interference was justified under Article 9(2) as a necessary safety measure.[1] The UN Human Rights Committee adopted a similar approach in its views in *K. Singh Bhinder v. Canada*[2] when it upheld the legitimacy of legislation requiring employees of the Federal-owned state railway company to wear protective headgear whilst at work. Prior to the Commission's decision in *X. v. the United Kingdom*, however, the United Kingdom had already decided to exempt Sikhs from this requirement by amending the Road Traffic Act expressly to exclude turban-wearing Sikhs from its scope of application and many states have adopted similar legislation with respect to head-gear in other contexts. For example, Canada subsequently permitted members of the Royal Canadian Mounted Police to wear turbans instead of the traditional stetson hat (this giving rise to a challenge before the Human Rights Committee from those opposed to such a change in *Riley v. Canada*,[3] which will be touched on later).

Although not expressed in these terms, whilst the human rights bodies have been prepared to accept the legitimacy of such restrictions on the basis that the state has a legitimate interest in ensuring the general health and safety of those

---

1   *X. v.* the *United Kingdom,* no . 7992/77, Commission decision of 12 July 1978, Decisions and Reports 14, p. 234.

2   *K. Singh Bhinder v. Canada,* Communication no. 208/1986 (views of 9 November 1989), UN Doc. A/45/40 vol. 2(1990), p. 50.

3   *Riley v. Canada,* Communication No. 1048/2002 (decision of 21 March 2002), UN Doc. A/57/40 Vol. 2 (2002), p. 256.

for whom it is responsible and is best placed to make that determination, in the absence of any evidence of unjustified direct or indirect discrimination, it is prepared to leave the striking of that balance to the state itself. If the state feels that it is able to make an adjustment in order to accommodate the needs of believers, then it is of course free to do so. However, it is then important that a similar consideration be given to the needs of all other similarly placed believers of other religious persuasions. Some care is needed in making this assessment since it might require some potentially controversial consideration of the nature of the beliefs at issue. For example, if turban-wearing Sikhs are permitted to ride motorcycles without wearing crash helmets, should headscarf- or Burqa-wearing Muslim women be allowed to do likewise? To exempt one group of believers but not another from the same legislative requirement without an objective and reasonable justification would be discriminatory. It is, however, possible to discern relevant differences, not least that is it is not impossible for a Muslim women to wear protective headgear whilst wearing her religiously inspired attire, whilst this is simply not the case for turban-wearing men. Though the drawing of such distinctions may not be welcome, it is both acceptable and, indeed, necessary and, once again, can only be undertaken in the light of the provision at issue and the believers and belief system in question.

Without being prescriptive, it is likely that there will be less scope for such accommodations to be made when the legislation at issue is not directed so much at the health and safety of the wearer, but at the protection of the health or safety of others. Thus restrictions on wearing or carrying forms of traditional weaponry which may have a religious significance to the bearer (such as ceremonial daggers or swords) may be legitimately restricted if this is considered necessary to preserve public safety and public order in situations in which others might reasonably be in fear of their safety, though once again it would be quite acceptable to seek to provide accommodations if this is possible.

(b) The example of public security

Unsurprisingly, there is likely to be little room for accommodation when issues of more general public security is at issue, as it shown by the decision of the Court in case of

Phull v. France. The applicant was a Sikh and was required
by his beliefs to wear a turban which security staff at
Entzheim Airport, Strasbourg, compelled him to remove
for the purposes of a routine security inspection when
entering the departure lounge. He argued that this had been
unnecessary, especially as he had gone through a walk-
through scanner and had been checked with a hand-held
detector. Nevertheless, the Court, quoting *X v. the United
Kingdom*, said:

> 'Firstly, security checks in airports are undoubtedly neces-
> sary in the interests of public safety within the meaning of
> that provision. Secondly, the arrangements for implementing
> them in the present case fell within the respondent state's
> margin of appreciation, particularly as the measure was only
> resorted to occasionally.'[4]

Thus the state is accorded a very broad margin of appreciation when issues of general public safety are at issue.
However, the manner in which the request to remove the
turban and the circumstances in which it might be removed
and the passenger screened are all matters which might be
taken into account in determining whether the interference
with the applicant's freedom of religion was proportionate. For example, it should be possible to arrange for such
checks to be carried out in private or relatively discreetly.
Similarly, it might be questioned whether an absolute ban
on the wearing of turbans, or of other forms of religiously
inspired attire, by air passengers would be as acceptable.

> The state is accorded a
> very broad margin of ap-
> preciation when issues of
> general public safety are
> at issue.

(c)   The question of 'public order'

This leads on to an altogether more controversial situation
in which the law restricts the wearing of particular forms of
religious symbols or attire in public altogether on the basis
that this is necessary for preserving public order. Although
the legitimacy of such prohibitions cannot be ruled out *a
priori*, it should be recalled that the Court has spoken out
in strong terms against any generalised linkages between
religious groups and violence threatening peace and security. In its decision in the case of *Norwood v. the United
Kingdom* the Court, when declining to allow the applicant
to proceed with a claim concerning his being convicted for

---

4   *Phull v. France* (dec.), no. 35753/03, ECHR 2005-I.

having put in his window a poster linking Islam with the 9/11 bombings, said that 'Such a general, vehement attack against a religious group, linking the group as a whole with a grave act of terrorism, is incompatible with the values proclaimed and guaranteed by the Convention, notably, tolerance, social peace and non-discrimination.'[5]

On the other hand, although in the case of the *Metropolitan Church of Bessarabia v. Moldova* the Court dismissed the state's argument that recognition of the applicant church would constitute a danger to national security and threaten its territorial integrity, it did so on the basis that this was 'a mere hypothesis which, *in the absence of corroboration*, cannot justify a refusal to recognise it.'[6] A similar approach was taken in the case of the *Moscow Branch of the Salvation Army v. Russia* where the Court, dismissing the claim that the applicant was to be likened to a 'paramilitary' organisation, said that restrictions on members of the Salvation Army for wearing military-style uniforms could not be justified, *inter alia*, because 'It could not seriously be maintained that [they] advocated a violent change of constitutional foundations or thereby undermined the integrity or security of the state. *No evidence to that effect had been produced*.'[7] In both these cases, then, the Court hints that restrictions on believers, including general restrictions on the wearing of religious symbols and clothing could be justifiable if there were a proper evidential basis to support that contention.

This approach finds some support in the judgment of the Grand Chamber of the Court in the case of *Refah Partisi* v. *Turkey*, where it said that:

> 'the acts and speeches of Refah's members and leaders cited by the Constitutional Court were imputable to the whole of the party, that those acts and speeches revealed Refah's long-term policy of setting up a regime based on sharia within the framework of a plurality of legal systems and that Refah did not exclude recourse to force in order to implement its policy and keep the system it envisaged in place. In view of the

---

5   *Norwood v. the United Kingdom* (dec.), op.cit.

6   *Metropolitan Church of Bessarabia and Others v. Moldova*, op.cit., para 126 (emphasis added).

7   *Moscow Branch of the Salvation Army v. Russia*, op.cit., para 92 (emphasis added).

fact that these plans were incompatible with the concept of a "democratic society" and that the real opportunities Refah had to put them into practice made the danger to democracy more tangible and more immediate, the penalty imposed on the applicants by the Constitutional Court .... may reasonably be considered to have met a "pressing social need".'[8]

Here, the Court carefully examined the material presented to it and found that it did indeed provide sufficient evidence of a threat sufficient to warrant restrictions being imposed, in this instance, upon a political party. Putting this together, it might be concluded that where there is solid and tangible evidence that a particular individual or religious group present a real and present danger to the security and integrity of a plural democratic society or to public security and safety, restrictions on the activities of religious believers may be permissible. Such restrictions may, of course, include restrictions on the display of religious symbols and the wearing of religious attire. Indeed, such restrictions may be required in such circumstances in order to preserve the rights and freedoms of others. As the Court said in the case of *97 Members of the Gldani Congregation* v. *Georgia,*

'... on account of their religious beliefs, which were considered unacceptable, the 96 applicants were attacked, humiliated and severely beaten during their congregation's meeting ... Having been treated in this way, the applicants were subsequently confronted with total indifference and a failure to act on the part of the authorities [which] ...opened the doors to a generalisation of religious violence throughout Georgia by the same group of attackers ... [T]hrough their inactivity, the relevant authorities failed in their duty to take the necessary measures to ensure that the group of Orthodox extremists .... tolerated the existence of the applicants' religious community and enabled them to exercise freely their rights to freedom of religion.'[9]

In circumstances such as these, the state is required to curb the excesses of religious believers and the use of proportionate restrictions on the wearing or display of religious symbols or clothing not only may offer a proportionate

---

8   *Refah Partisi (the Welfare Party) and* Others v. *Turkey* [GC], op.cit., para 132.

9   *Case of 97 Members of the Gldani Congregation of Jehovah's Witnesses and Others v. Georgia,* op.cit., paras 133- 134.

means of doing so but may also provide a means of giving effect to the state's obligation to ensure that believers tolerate each other.

Of course, general restrictions on the wearing of religious symbols can only be justified against an objectively discernable and specific danger. The wearing of a religious symbol or attire is not only an exercise of the freedom of religion or belief, it is also an exercise of the freedom of expression and in a classic statement of the scope of that right the Court has said that the freedom of expression 'is applicable not only to 'information' or ideas' that are favourably received or regarded as inoffensive or as a matter of indifference, but also those that offend, shock or disturb the state or any sector of the population. Such as the demands of that pluralism, tolerance and broadmindedness without which there is no 'democratic' society.[10] It follows from this that it is unacceptable to place general restrictions on the display of certain forms of symbols or attire simply because sections of the population find them unwelcome or offensive. Christian Nuns wearing full length habits and headgear in public places may offend some sections of the community, as might the wearing of saffron robes by male followers of Hare Krishna and both may appear out of kilter with the prevailing *mores* of a secular society. That, however, provides no more reason for restricting such forms of dress in public than would a prevailing religious ethos within society justify the imposition of dress codes forbidding the showing of parts of the body, the face or hair in public.

> It may be necessary for the state to take steps to preserve public order. However, rarely will general restrictions focussed upon the wearing or display of religious symbols or attire be compatible with Convention principles.

It may be concluded that the Court clearly recognises that it may be necessary for the state to take steps to preserve public order in situations where the display of religious symbolism places it under threat. However, rarely will general restrictions focussed upon the wearing or display of religious symbols or attire be compatible with Convention principles. Such limitations may be justified – or even required – in order to address well evidenced and specific concerns but these are likely to persist for only a limited period of time and in relation to particular situations and the restrictions should be similarly modulated.

---

10   *Handyside v. the United Kingdom,* op.cit., para 48.

There are, however, a range of particular contexts in which more general restrictions may be legitimate and a number of these will be explored in the sections which follow.

(B) The Wearing of Religious Symbols by those in General State Employment

The first of these contexts concerns those in state employment. The range of situations in which issues concerning the wearing of religious symbols might arise is of course enormous and maps onto the nature of the functions which each state considers appropriate to perform, as opposed to those it considers appropriate to regulate. Some of these relate to specific contexts and give rise to particular issues which will be considered separately. The concern at this point is for those in the general service of the state, rather than teachers, doctors, etc. It is axiomatic that an individual cannot be dismissed from their employment because of their beliefs.

As usual, the starting point must be that individual employees are free to manifest their religion or belief through the wearing of religious clothing or artefacts but this may be subject to restrictions which are in accordance with Article 9(2). At one level, it is arguably difficult to see why it is necessary for the state to restrict the wearing of religious symbols or clothing of its employees at all: if they are not fulfilling their contractual obligations in a satisfactory manner, or abusing their position as servants of the state in order to project their beliefs, then relevant action may be taken against them. If they are fulfilling their duties as state servants in an appropriate fashion, then it might be argued that unless there are more particular reasons for intervention, then restrictions cannot be justified. This approach was confirmed in the context of political beliefs in the case of *Vogt v. Germany*,[11] a case brought under Article 10, in which applicant had been dismissed from her employment as a teacher (a civil service position in Germany) as a result of her being an active member of the communist party, albeit it that this had no impact on her work as a teacher. In the case of *Ivanova v. Bulgaria*, the Court was faced with a similar situation, and in which it found that the applicant, a

---

11   *Vogt v. Germany*, judgment of 26 September 1995, Series A no, 323.

swimming pool attendant at a state run school, had lost her job because of her religious beliefs and this amounted to a violation of Article 9, 'there being no credible accusations that the applicant had proselytised at the School.'[12] In the *Vogt* case, the Court summed up the relevant approach in the following terms:

> 'Although it is legitimate for a state to impose on civil servants, on account of their status, a duty of discretion, civil servants are individuals and, as such, qualify for the protection of Article 10 of the Convention. It therefore falls to the Court, having regard to the circumstances of each case, to determine whether a fair balance has been struck between the fundamental right of the individual to freedom of expression and the legitimate interest of a democratic state in ensuring that its civil service properly furthers the purposes enumerated in Article 10 para. 2. In carrying out this review, the Court will bear in mind that whenever civil servants' right to freedom of expression is in issue the 'duties and responsibilities' referred to in Article 10 para. 2 assume a special significance, which justifies leaving to the national authorities a certain margin of appreciation in determining whether the impugned interference is proportionate to the above aim.'[13]

The Court has made it clear that the same approach is to be taken in cases concerning Article 9, stressing that in such cases it may be necessary to accept an even greater margin of appreciation in determining how that balance is to be struck.[14]

Whilst this is true, it is equally the case that the state must be neutral and impartial and in many of its dealings it will, through its employees, come into contact with believers of many faith traditions and of none. It is, then, legitimate to seek to ensure that the public-fronting 'face of the state' does not project a particular religious ethos if this is considered necessary to protect the rights and freedoms of others by ensuring that there is general confidence that the state is acting in an objective and even-handed fashion in its functional capacity.

---

12   *Ivanova v. Bulgaria*, no. 52435/99, para 82, ECHR 2007.
13   *Vogt v. Germany*, op.cit., para 53.
14   See *Kurtulmuş v. Turkey* (dec.), no. 65500/01, ECHR 2006-II.

However, this does not mean that all state employees need be subjected to such restrictions. Rather, it means that the context needs to be considered in order to see whether it is necessary for the state to ensure that a neutral and impartial image is presented in the situation in question. Certainly, a general appeal to 'secularism' is unlikely to be sufficient to justify a general restriction upon state employees manifesting their beliefs in dress: for example, in *Ivanova v. Bulgaria*,[15] the Court rejected the Government's argument that the secular nature of the education system in Bulgaria justified the limitation on a person's freedom of religion *per se*. At the other end of the spectrum, in the case of *Kalaç v. Turkey*,[16] the Court made it clear that when a judicial function is at issue, the state is certainly entitled to take steps to ensure the absence of any perception of religiously motivated bias, and this could extend to the wearing of religious symbols by members of the judiciary and those employed in the court services. It is, then, appropriate to focus on the function of the state employee rather than on the fact of state employment when determining the legitimacy of any restriction.

If one takes this approach, there is an immediate distinction to be drawn between those who through their employment come into direct contact with the public and those who do not. Many state employees work in closed working environments, such as accountants, managers, administrators, general office staff, building service workers, etc and do not come into contact with the public in the natural course of their day to day work. It is more difficult to justify restrictions on the wearing of religious symbols in such contexts. The potential impact of such symbols is limited and primarily affects relations between the employees themselves who, understanding the nature of their mutual employment, might reasonably be expected to respect the choices of their colleagues provided this does not impact on their working relationships. Although one cannot dismiss the possibility that the mere fact of wearing a religious symbol may be inimical to the ethos of state employment, and so justify a restriction, this would need very careful and critical scrutiny.

> Although one cannot dismiss the possibility that the mere fact of wearing a religious symbol may be inimical to the ethos of state employment, and so justify a restriction, this would need very careful and critical scrutiny.

---

15 *Ivanova v. Bulgaria*, no. 52435/99, ECHR 2007.
16 *Kalaç v. Turkey*, op.cit.

For those whose state employment brings them into regular contact with the public, a greater range of restrictions may be justifiable. Since those of all faiths and of none may be required to have dealings with a wide range of state employees there may be a greater need to ensure that the neutrality and impartiality of the state in matters of religion or belief is manifested in the manner in which those servants present themselves to the general public. This would apply not only to those working in the public space, such as the police, but those who provide services in the community, such as health and social workers, and also those who fulfil public-facing functions in official buildings, such as receptionists, etc. Once again, neutrality and impartiality does not demand that this be the case, but it is within the margin of appreciation of the state to determine that this be so. For example, it might reasonably be decided that it would be inappropriate for a social worker to conduct a visit wearing religious symbols or clothing and so be the subject of a legitimate restriction since it could inhibit his or her ability to properly fulfil their professional functions. However, in some situations, it may well facilitate the performance of that function by encouraging an empathetic relationship, particularly where minorities and vulnerable groups are involved. Of course, even then there is a proportionality requirement and it may be that a religious symbol or item of clothing may be so obviously a personal matter that it could not reasonably be considered to be associated with the official persona of the state employee. Thus whilst one would not expect to see a religious symbol on a police car or an ambulance, it may be quite reasonable for a social worker to have a religious symbol or sticker on a privately owned vehicle even if it were being used in the course of their employment to visit members of the public.

The sheer number of variety of settings makes it impossible to consider them all. However, more will be said about two particular contexts since they underline some of the complexities involved.

(a) Hospitals and medical services.

The origins of many medical facilities lie in the voluntary sector and a large number of these were originally religious foundations, a fact that often remains reflected in their very names. It is axiomatic that state-provided medical services must be available on a non-discriminatory basis and must not be offered under the guise of religion, though this does not mean that it is necessary to abandon or deny the heritage of its provenance. Nor does it mean that the state may not take advantage of the continued volunteer contributions of those offering their assistance and service as an action motivated by their religious beliefs. It also flows from what has already been said that medical workers must properly fulfil their professional roles and must not allow their personal beliefs to influence their clinical judgement or affect the carrying out of their professional responsibilities. For example, it was already seen that the Court rejected a claim made by Catholics working in a pharmacy in France that they ought not be required to dispense contraceptives.[17] It may similarly be expected that medical workers may be required to refrain from wearing religious symbols or clothing which might legitimately cause the sick and the vulnerable, and their relatives, to be apprehensive as to their professionalism and objectivity. This does not mean that a person of a given religious persuasion may be barred from some medical roles: what it does mean is that if those of a given religious view choose to be employed in such a position, then they might expect to be required to act in accordance with the relevant professional standards rather than with their personal belief systems, should the two differ in any respect.[18]

At the same time, it is recognised that as places of healing and caring, hospitals must cater for the spiritual as well as physical needs of those patients which desire it. To that end, the state may employ, or permit access to, clergy or other religious personnel and it goes without saying that, since their function is religious in nature then there ought to be no restriction upon their wearing or displaying religious clothing or symbols: it is what they are there to do. It is equally clear that the demands of state neutrality and impartiality does not extend to preventing patients from

---

17 *Pichon and Sajous v. France* (dec.), op.cit.

18 It may, of course, be possible for the respective positions to be reconciled through the use of sympathetic practical arrangements since there is no need to compel public servants to undertake tasks which run counter to their conscientiously held beliefs. Indeed, the demands of pluralism and tolerance may require that these options be explored. In the face of fundamental conflict, however, the position remains as stated.

displaying religious symbols which may be a comfort to them, though some restrictions may be necessary in order to ensure mutual respect and the rights and freedoms of others from time to time in particular situations where such symbols may impede the recovery or quietude of other patients.

It is clear that the complexities of the medical setting preclude the application of a rigid approach to the wearing of religious symbols by both employees and by patients and that specific issues can only be resolved in the light of the principles identified in the earlier sections of this Manual.

(b) Military settings

A similar range of issues applies in the military setting. The Court made it clear as long ago as the *Engel* case[19] that, whilst certainly able to benefit from the enjoyment of Convention rights, members of the armed forces might expect to be subject to a greater number of limitations than civilians. Thus in the case of *Kalaç v. Turkey*, the Court noted that 'in exercising his freedom to manifest his religion, an individual may need to take his specific situation into account' and that 'In choosing to pursue a military career Mr Kalaç was accepting of his own accord a system of military discipline that by its very nature implied the possibility of placing on certain of the rights and freedoms of members of the armed forces limitations incapable of being imposed on civilians. States may adopt for their armies disciplinary regulations forbidding this or that type of conduct, in particular an attitude inimical to an established order reflecting the requirements of military service'.[20]

Once again, this legitimates placing restriction on the wearing of religious symbols but it does not *require* that there be such restrictions. Once again, this falls within the margin of appreciation of the state and its decision must be consonant with the concepts of neutrality and impartiality. Given the security function of the armed forces, the need for them to project the values of pluralism and tolerance are likely to merit particular weight and it is clear from the case-law

---

19   *Engel and Others v. the Netherlands*, judgment of 8 June 1976, Series A no. 22.

20   *Kalaç v. Turkey*, op.cit., paras 27-28.

of the UN Human Rights Committee that the wearing of religious symbols or clothing is not necessarily inimical to the military function when doing so reflects the personal beliefs of the members of the armed forces, rather than a manifestation of the ethos of the military as an institution. Thus in its views in *Riley* v. *Canada*[21] the Human Rights Committee rejected the argument put forward by the applicant that the wearing of a turban by a member of the Royal Canadian Mounted Police (the 'Mounties') would both raise an apprehension of bias in the minds of civilians and also that, since the state should be secular, it was a violation of their Covenant right to freedom of religion or belief to have the security forces of the state present a religious face. By deciding that the wearing of religious symbols by security forces did not interfere with the rights of the applicant, the Committee in effect rejected the legitimacy of both these arguments.

As in the hospital settings, the state may also employ staff to minister to the spiritual needs of its security forces and such staff will, as a natural consequence of their functions, wear and display religious clothing and symbols in the course of their employment without in any sense raising questions regarding the neutrality or impartiality of the state. This would only be at issue if the state were to respond to the spiritual welfare of only one group of its employees and the principles of non-discrimination requires that the legitimate needs of all its servants be met in this fashion. The closed nature of the armed forces, particularly in operational settings, means that there may be no alternative source of religious services available to the serving soldier. This makes it all the more important that the state offer that provision in order to ensure that military personnel can enjoy their freedom of religion or belief, whilst recognising that where military service is voluntary, the scope for legitimate restrictions on the enjoyment of the right will be greater than in those instances in which it is not.

---

21   *Riley v. Canada*, op.cit.

(C) The Wearing of Religious Symbols in Public Educational Institutions

The context in which the wearing of religious symbols and clothing has received the most attention is that of public[22] educational institutions. In many states, education is not only directly provided by the state but is also provided in privately run educational institutions under a general regulatory scheme. Moreover, state education may sometimes be directly provided through educational facilities provided by private bodies, many of which are religious in origins or remain religious in both name and ethos. In the light of this diversity of approach within member states of the Council of Europe, and the diversity of provision available within each state itself, it is to be expected that the state will enjoy a considerable margin of appreciation in determining the balance to be struck between the right of the individual to manifest their religion or belief and the need to protect the rights and freedoms of others and to avoid such institutions becoming places of indoctrination rather than of education.

In conducting this balancing act, the state must be mindful of the need to be neutral and impartial in its approach, but at the same time it should be acting in a fashion with encourages pluralism and tolerance. The tension between these latter considerations is particularly problematic in the educational context. On the one hand, children and young adults need to be free to make up their own minds on matters of belief, yet in order to do so they need to be introduced to those beliefs and receive an education which, whilst not biassed in favour or against a particular form of religious belief or for or against religion in general, acknowledges the role of religion in the life of believers and its relationship with democratic pluralism. It is helpful to

In the light of this diversity of approach within member states of the Council of Europe, the state will enjoy a considerable margin of appreciation in determining the balance to be struck between the right of the individual to manifest their religion or belief and the need to protect the rights and freedoms of others and to avoid schools becoming places of indoctrination rather than of education.

---

22   In many Council of Europe countries it is impossible to make a clear distinction between public and private schools. A 'public school' refers to a school whose organisation, financing and management are primarily the responsibility of, or under the primary oversight of, a public body (state, regional, municipal, etc). A 'private' school is a school in which, irrespective of whether it may receive degrees of support (including financial support) from public sources, matters of organisation, financing and management are primarily the responsibility of the School itself, or of a non- public sponsoring body. (Definition adapted from the OSCE's *Toledo Guiding Principles on Teaching about Religions and Belief in Public Schools* (2007)).

consider the situation of teachers and pupils separately and different considerations are relevant.

(a) The teacher

The teacher, as an individual, enjoys the freedom of thought, conscience and religion and teachers may manifest their religion or belief in accordance with the general human rights framework. It is also axiomatic that teachers must approach their task in a balanced and professional fashion and must not exploit their teaching position to impose personal beliefs that are inconsistent with conscientious beliefs of their pupils. Being in a position of authority over children and young people may give their views a particular weight. Moreover, by virtue of their having chosen to work in an educational environment, a range of restrictions may legitimately be placed upon teachers when they are working in the classroom in order to ensure that an educational environment appropriate to the school in question is maintained and that the human rights of parents and children are respected.

The manner in which these factors come together is illustrated by the case of *Dahlab v. Switzerland*. The application was a primary School teacher and a convert to Islam who, after having worn a headscarf at work without this occasioning any comment for a number of years was asked to stop doing so in order to ensure that the religious beliefs of pupils and parents were respected, it being argued that this was undermined by a teacher wearing a 'powerful religious symbol ... Directly recognisable by others'. The applicant contested this, arguing, *inter alia*, that the mere fact of wearing a headscarf was not likely to influence the children's beliefs. In a passage which merits being reproduced at length, the Court said that

> 'it is very difficult to assess the impact that a powerful external symbol such as the wearing of a headscarf may have on the freedom of conscience and religion of very young children. The applicant's pupils were aged between four and eight, an age at which children wonder about many things and are also more easily influenced than older pupils. In those circumstances, it cannot be denied outright that the wearing of a headscarf might have some kind of proselytising effect .... It therefore appears difficult to reconcile the wear-

ing of an Islamic headscarf with the message of tolerance, respect for others and, above all, equality and non-discrimination that all teachers in a democratic society must convey to their pupils.

Accordingly, weighing the right of a teacher to manifest her religion against the need to protect pupils by preserving religious harmony, the Court considers that, in the circumstances of the case and having regard, above all, to the tender age of the children for whom the applicant was responsible as a representative of the state, the Geneva authorities did not exceed their margin of appreciation and that the measure they took was therefore not unreasonable.[23]

Is the balance to be struck in a different fashion when the teaching of older children or young adults is at issue? Much will depend on the contextual circumstances but, once again, the state has a wide margin of appreciation in determining the necessity of any restriction. For example, in *Kurtulmus* v. *Turkey*[24] the Court dismissed an application from an associate professor at Istanbul University who had been subjected to disciplinary procedures for wearing a headscarf at work, endorsing the approach adopted in the *Dahlab* case and in the case of *Leyla Şahin* v. *Turkey*,[25] considered below. Given the particular sensitivity of the educational context, teachers may legitimately be subjected to restrictions upon their wearing religious symbols and clothing by the state, provided this can be shown to be compatible with the underlying ethos of the educational system, is applied in a non-discriminatory fashion and is a proportionate response on the facts of the case. In determining whether such restrictions are legitimate, the principles of respect and tolerance must also be taken into account.

(b) Students

The importance of the principles of toleration and respect also explains the significance of the increasingly important issue of whether children can manifest their religious beliefs

---

23 *Dahlab v. Switzerland* (dec.), no. 42393/98, ECHR 2001-V.

24 *Kurtulmuş v. Turkey* (dec.), no. 65500/01, ECHR 2006-II.

25 *Leyla Şahin v. Turkey* [GC], *ibid.*, para 109.

through the wearing of religiously inspired clothing or symbols while attending lessons, and whether restrictions on such clothing or symbols are compatible with the notion of 'respect'. Once again, the resolution of such questions must depend on the facts of each case, but it will always remain important to ensure that any restrictions placed upon the manifestation of religion or belief by pupils are strictly necessary and in the pursuit of legitimate aims of public safety, health, order, or the protection of the rights and freedoms of others, the latter informed by the importance of fostering a tolerant and inclusive educational environment.

A further complexity is that the younger the child, the greater may be the impact of preventing that child from wearing a symbol or item of clothing which they habitually wear as they may be less able to understand the effect which it might have on others and the reasonableness of a restriction in the interests of fostering mutual tolerance, such understandings being more accessible to the older child or young adult.

In the *Dahlab* case, for example, the Government made it clear that the prohibition on religious symbols and clothing did not extend to pupils, as they did not think this was necessary in order to maintain the secular nature of its schools and to preserve the separation of church and state. In the case of *Leyla Şahin v. Turkey*, however, the Court accepted that such restrictions might legitimately be placed on students at University if this were motivated by the desire to uphold the secular nature of the institution (the assessment of whether this was necessary largely being a matter that fell within the margin of appreciation of the state). Endorsing the position of the state, in its judgment the Court said 'it is the principle of secularism ... which is the paramount consideration underlying the ban on the wearing of religious symbols in universities. In such a context, where the values of pluralism, respect for the rights of other and, in particular equality before the law of men and women are being taught and applied in practice, it is understandable that the relevant authorities should wish to preserve the secular nature of the institution considered and so consider it contrary to such values to allow religious attire'.[26] The Court subsequently adopted the same approach in upholding the legitimacy of a ban on headscarves imposed on

26   *Leyla Şahin v. Turkey* [GC], op.cit., para 116.

younger teenagers at a lycée in Istanbul in the case of *Köse and others v. Turkey*.[27]

Restrictions, then, may be imposed upon pupils as well as teachers. There is, however, an additional factor to be taken into account. Attendance at schools is usually compulsory. Moreover, it may not be possible to avoid a prohibition on the wearing of religious symbols and clothing in one institution by the expedient of moving to a different institution where different rules might apply. For example, in the domestic case of *R (ex parte Begum) v. Denbigh High School*[28] a number of UK judges in the House of Lords took the view that there had been no interference with the applicants' freedom of religion which was attributable to the state since although the School's uniform policy did not permit her to wear a jilbab to School, there were other Schools that she might have transferred to which would have allowed her to do so. They were, however, clear that had there been no alternative, matters would have been different (although on the facts of the case the Court was still of the view that had there been an interference attributable to the state then it would have been justified). Where the state compels attendance at secular institutions and prohibits in absolute terms the wearing of religious symbols and clothing, there is an enhanced danger that this will itself foster intolerance of religious diversity and inhibit the advancement of pluralism, and so particular care must be taken when exercising European scrutiny of the domestic margin of appreciation to ensure that the core convention principles of democracy, respect, pluralism and tolerance are being properly reflected in the regulatory scheme.

(c) Administrators and others

Schools are places of work for many besides teachers and pupils, such as administrators, secretaries, cooks, caretakers, cleaners, etc and their position was touched upon in the case of *Ivanova v. Bulgaria*. The applicant was a swimming pool manager at a school and also a member of the 'Word of Life', a Christian Evangelical group. Following a change in leadership at the school the job description for

---

27 *Köse and Others v. Turkey* (dec.), op.cit.

28 *R (ex parte Begum) v. Denbigh High School*, [2006] UKHL 15; [2007] 1 AC 100.

her post was rewritten and she was subsequently dismissed from her post. The Court ultimately decided that she had been dismissed on account of her unwillingness to abandon her religious beliefs and that this amounted to coercion and thus violated Article 9. In the course of argument the respondent state had suggested that 'the secular nature of the system of education .... applied both to the teaching activities of the School and to its premises'.[29] Although the case did not address the issue of non teaching staff wearing religious clothing or symbols, the Court did make reference to the previous decisions is cases such as *Knudsen v. Norway*,[30] *Konttinen v. Finland*[31] and *Vogt v. Germany*[32] saying that these cases showed that 'In the context of complaints under article 9 ... for dismissal from service ... pressuring an individual to change his religious beliefs or preventing him from manifesting them would be an interference'.[33] This suggests that the principles to be applied in such cases will be those outlined in the previous section concerning state employees and that whilst the educational context is relevant to that determination, it does not preclude the wearing of such clothing and such symbols *per se*. Nor should it be assumed that limitations which might be appropriately placed upon teachers with prolonged direct contact with students would necessarily be appropriate for those whose work is ancillary to the teaching role.

(D) The Private Sector

The previous sections have focussed on the public sector but the issues addressed above will also arise in the context of the private sector. Where the private sector is being used by the state to fulfil what would otherwise be state functions – such as the use of private security guards to transport prisoners – then the same considerations as are relevant to the public sector will apply in equal measure and no further examination is necessary. There are, however, two particular areas which do require further considera-

---

29   *Ivanova v. Bulgaria*, op.cit, para 74.
30   *Knudsen v. Norway*, op.cit.
31   *Konttinen v. Finland*, op.cit.
32   *Vogt v. Germany*, op.cit.
33   *Ivanova v. Bulgaria*, op.cit., para 80.

tion, these being general employment in the private sector
and private education.

(a) *General private sector employment*

Although the state is not directly responsible for the actions
of private employers, those working in the private sector
remain free to enjoy their freedom of religion or belief and
the state is obliged to ensure that restrictions that might
be placed upon them by their employers are compatible
with convention standards. Private sector employment is of
course subject to the general provisions of employment law
which, as a form of law which is of general application, may
be the source of legitimate restrictions upon the wearing of
religious symbols in the workplace. The scope of such laws
has been considered above and does not need to be repeated here. Likewise, it is beyond the scope of this Manual
to consider the compatibility of employment law in general
with Convention standards. Nevertheless, private employment is very different to state employment. Whilst private
employers must conform to laws of general application, they
are not bound to project the values of neutrality, respect
and tolerance in the same manner as the state. Provided that
they are operating within the parameters set by the more
general legal framework, they may encourage and promote
the wearing of religious symbols or clothing if they consider
this appropriate (as might many religious or religiously
inspired organisations). Likewise, private employers might
choose to restrict their employees from doing so if they
wish- again, provided that this is within the limits provided
by law for the proper protection of the rights of employees,
including human rights protections and anti-discrimination
legislation. In other words, private employers enjoy a greater
degree of latitude when formulating their policies on religious symbols and clothing in the workplace than is the case
within the public sector, provided that the result remains
compatible with domestic law. The reason for this is twofold:
first, the employee's freedom of religion and belief is considered to be adequately protected by their right to terminate
their contract of employment, as illustrated by those cases
concerning time off work for attendance at services or wor-

> Those working in the private sector remain free to enjoy their freedom of religion or belief and the state is obliged to ensure that restrictions that might be placed upon them by their employers are compatible with convention standards.

ship or religious festivals.[34] Second, there is not the same need to maintain 'neutrality' in the private workplace and in the delivery of private services as there is in the public sector and in the delivery of public services.[35]

(b) Private education

It has already been pointed out that many educational institutions are religious in origin. The close intermingling of education and faith-based institutions in a considerable number of Council of Europe states has resulted in a situation in which many public educational establishments are run by faith traditions. Although faith-inspired, they nevertheless remain part of the public educational system and so are subject to the same considerations as have been considered above. In many countries, however, there are alternatives to the public educational system in the form of private schools, many of which are also faith based, either in origin or in their contemporary ethos and orientation. Since Article 2 of the first protocol to the ECHR expressly enjoins states, to 'respect the right of parents to ensure such education and teaching in conformity with their own religious and philosophical convictions' in the 'exercise of any functions which it assumes in relation to education and to teaching', it might be argued that in the private educational sector there is even greater freedom for schools to pursue their own approaches. Moreover, and by analogy with private sector employment, since no-one is compelled to attend private schools this further re-enforces their ability to adopt approaches to religious symbols and religious clothing which might differ from those in the public sector: if parents choose to send their children to a privately run school which has a clear policy with regard to religiously

---

34 See, for example, *Stedman v. the United Kingdom*, op.cit., and *Kosteski v. the former Yugoslav Republic of Macedonia*, op.cit., para 39.

35 It is important to note that different considerations may apply in situations where private employers might seek to insist upon employees being adherents of a particular faith, or insist on their wearing religious clothing in order to be offered a contract of employment in the first place. The comments made here relate only to the situation in which an employee seeks to exercise a personal wish to wear a religious symbol or religiously inspired clothing, and is prevented from doing so by a corporate policy.

inspired attire, then that is a matter for them – indeed, it might be the very reason why they choose to do so.

Both of these arguments are only valid to a limited degree. The Court has made it clear that the state remains responsible for the conduct of private as well as public schools. For example, in a case concerning the use of corporal punishment in a private school in the United Kingdom, the government argued that 'whilst ... the state exercised a limited degree of control and supervision over independent schools ... the Government denied that they were directly responsible for every aspect of the way in which they were run; in particular, they assumed no function in matters of discipline'.[36] The Court rejected this, noting first that 'the state has an obligation to secure children their right to education under Article 2 of Protocol No. 1' and that ' ... Functions relating to the internal administration of a school, such as discipline, cannot be said to be merely ancillary to the educational process'.[37] Secondly, it observed that 'in the United Kingdom, independent schools co-exist with a system of public education' and so 'the fundamental right of everyone to education is a right guaranteed equally to pupils in state and independent schools, no distinction being made between the two'.[38] It also noted that 'the state cannot absolve itself from responsibility by delegating its obligations to private bodies or individuals'.[39] In the light of this, the Court concluded that 'in the present case, which relates to the particular domain of school discipline, the treatment complained of, although it was the act of a head-master of an independent school, is none the less such as may engage the responsibility of the United Kingdom under the Convention'.[40]

As school dress codes are seen as intimately linked to more general questions of school order and governance it seems clear that the Court would be prepared to consider the responsibility of the state engaged were such policies inimical

36   *Costello-Roberts v. the United Kingdom*, judgment of 25 March 1993, Series A no, 247-C, para 25.

37   *Ibid*, para 27.

38   *Ibid*, quoting *Kjeldsen, Busk Madsen and Pederson* v. *Denmark*, op.cit., para 50.

39   *Ibid*, quoting *Van der Mussele v. Belgium*, judgment of 23 November 1983, Series A no. 70, paras 28-30.

40   *Ibid*, para 28.

to the overarching Convention values which the state education system must promote. Thus, just as within the state
system itself, there will be a margin or appreciation which
may be exercised in such a way as to allow for a proper
balancing of the ethos of the institution with the need to
ensure that children are educated in an environment which
properly respects the freedom of religion and belief of all. In
conclusion, it can be said that whilst the nuance of application may differ, there is no fundamental difference in the
approaches to be applied between the public and the private educational sectors, since the Court has made it clear
that there are no 'bright lines' to be drawn between them as
regards the application of the Convention.

(E) The Wearing of Religious Symbols and the Criminal Justice System

A final area which merits particular consideration concerns
the criminal justice system. Some of the very earliest cases
involving the freedom of religion and belief considered under the Convention system concerned the rights of prisoners and there is increasing interest in how religious authorities respond to the perceived requirements of religious
believers at all phases of the criminal justice process. We
are not concerned here with the wearing of religious symbols or religiously inspired clothing by members of the law
enforcement agencies or the presence of religious symbols
in police stations, courts and prisons. Since such personnel are state employees (or are to be considered as state
employees) exercising a quintessential state function, the
principles already considered above will apply. Rather, we
are concerned with the situation of those who are brought
into contact with the criminal justice system, as suspects,
witnesses, the accused and the convicted.

The starting point must be that such individuals enjoy the
right to manifest their religion or belief and this includes
the wearing of religious symbols or clothing in exactly the
same fashion as anyone else. We have, however, already
seen that this may be restricted in the interests of national
security and it is reasonable to permit the security forces
to insist on the removal of religiously inspired symbols
and clothing where this is necessary on security grounds.[41]

---

41   See, for example, *Phull v. France* (dec.), op.cit.

This may reasonably be extended to situations in which it is necessary in order to secure the proper administration of justice, both in court and in the execution of custodial sentences. In practice, this is likely to mean that there is something of a 'sliding scale'. For example, it may be necessary to allow the security forces to remove objects or items of clothing in order to take a person into custody if they are resisting arrest, or if it hampers identification. This, however, is likely to be a temporary expedient and should not be prolonged for longer than is strictly necessary.

Whilst a person is in pre-trial detention, the European Prison Rules expressly provide that 'Untried Prisoners shall be allowed to wear their own clothing if it is suitable for wearing in prison'[42] and when a case comes to Court, there is no general need to prevent the accused and witnesses from displaying religious symbols or wearing religiously-inspired clothing unless this threatens the integrity of the judicial process. For example, it may be that by displaying a particular religious symbol or by wearing religious clothing an individual might be attempting to influence the court in their favour, making it more difficult to secure a conviction or to discount their evidence. Under such circumstances, a restriction may be justifiable. Likewise, where religious clothing may make identification or communication difficult, or prevent a person's response to questioning from being observed (and thereby hampering the fair conduct of a case), restrictions may again be justifiable.

Once a person has been convicted of an offence and sentenced to a term of imprisonment, limitations upon their ability to wear religious symbols or clothing become progressively more difficult to justify, though the nature of prison life may inevitably require a greater degree of limitation than would otherwise be acceptable. The UN Human Rights Committee has said that 'persons already subject to certain legitimate constraints, such as prisoners, continue to enjoy their rights to manifest their religion or belief to the fullest extent compatible with the specific nature of the constraint.'[43] The difficultly lies in assessing that degree of compatibility. In assessing the legitimacy of such restrictions a strict approach to their necessity is needed and

---

42   Recommendation Rec(2006)2 of the Committee of Ministers to member states on the European Prison Rules, Rule 97(1).

43   UN HRC General Comment No. 22, para 8.

regard should be had to the European Prison Rules which provide in regard of sentenced prisoners that 'Prisoners' freedom of thought, conscience and religion shall be respected' and 'The prison regime shall be organised so far as is practicable to allow prisoners to practice their religion and follow their beliefs.'[44]

> It is not permitted under any circumstances to use the removal of, or restrictions upon, the wearing of religious symbols or clothing as a means of coercing or punishing a suspect, witness or prisoner.

In its early jurisprudence, the European Commission on Human Rights took a fairly robust approach, seemingly willing to justify restrictions on prisoners having access to religious artefacts or following religiously-inspired modes of personal attire on relatively insubstantial grounds. For example, in one very early case the Commission accepted that 'public order' considerations justified the prison authorities' refusal to allow a practising Buddhist to grow a beard on the grounds that it would hinder identification.[45] In a subsequent case, the Commission concluded that there had been no violation of Article 9 where a Sikh had been required to wear prison clothing which, he claimed, violated his religious beliefs (albeit on the grounds that this claim was not substantiated).[46] It is likely that a somewhat stricter approach would be taken by the Court today, as it has been by the UN Human Rights Committee which considered the forced removal of the beard of a Muslim prisoner to violate his freedom of religion or belief.[47] One thing is, however, absolutely clear. It is not permitted under any circumstances to use the removal of, or restrictions upon, the wearing of religious symbols or clothing as a means of coercing or punishing a suspect, witness or prisoner. Indeed, the removal of religious symbols or clothing might amount to a form of 'inhuman or degrading' treatment or punishment and render the state in breach of Article 3 of the ECHR.

---

44 Recommendation Rec(2006)2 of the Committee of Ministers to member states on the European Prison Rules, Rule 29(1) and (2).

45 *X v. Austria*, no. 1753/63, Commission decision, 1965, Yearbook of the European Commission on Human Rights 8, p. 184.

46 *X v. the United Kingdom*, no. 8231/78, Commission decision of 6 March 1982, Decisions and Reports 28, p. 5 at p. 27. The European Prison Rules do not require or preclude that sentenced prisoners be made to wear prison uniform, but they do require that any such prison clothing 'shall not be degrading or humiliating', Recommendation Rec(2006)2 of the Committee of Ministers to member states on the European Prison Rules, Rule 20(2).

47 *Boodoo v. Trinidad and Tobago*, Communication no. 721/1997 (views of 2 August 2002, UN doc. A/57/40, vol 2 (2002), p. 76.

annexes

Relevant Applicable international Human Rights Instruments

Relevant Rights / Instruments	Freedom of religion and to manifest one's religion	Prohibition of discrimination based on religion	Freedom of expression	Right to education	Respect for private life
Universal Declaration of Human Rights	– Article 18 – Article 29 (conditions for limitations to be acceptable)	– Article 2 – Article 7	Article 19	Article 26	Article 12
International Covenant on Civil and Political Rights[1]	– Article 18 – Article 27	Article 26	Article 19		Article 17
International Covenant on Economic, Social and Cultural Rights[2]				Article 13	
European Convention on Human Rights[3]	Article 9	– Article 14 – Article 1, Protocol No. 12	Article 10	Article 2, Protocol No. 1	Article 8
European Social Charter (revised)[4]		Article E			
Framework Convention for the Protection of National Minorities[5]	– Article 5 – Article 7 – Article 8	Article 4	Article 9	Article 12	
UN Declaration on the Elimination of All forms of Intolerance and of Discrimination Based on Religion or Belief	– Article 1 – Article 6				

1   The International Covenant on Civil and Political Rights is legally
     binding on all member states.
2   The International Covenant on Economic, Social and Cultural
     Rights is legally binding on all member states.
3   Protocol No. 1 to the ECHR has been ratified by all member states
     except Andorra, Monaco and Switzerland. Protocol No. 12 to the
     ECHR has been ratified by the following member states: Albania,
     Armenia, Bosnia and Herzegovina, Croatia, Cyprus, Finland,
     Georgia, Luxembourg, Netherlands, Romania, San Marino, Ser-
     bia, "the former Yugoslav Republic of Macedonia", Ukraine.
4   The European Social Charter (revised) has been ratified by the
     following member states: Albania, Andorra, Armenia, Azerbaijan,
     Belgium, Bulgaria, Cyprus, Estonia, Finland, France, Georgia,
     Ireland, Italy, Lithuania, Malta, Moldova, Netherlands, Norway,
     Portugal, Romania, Slovenia, Sweden.
5   The Framework Convention on the Protection of National Mi-
     norities has been ratified by all member states except Andorra,
     Belgium, France, Greece, Iceland, Luxembourg, Monaco and
     Turkey.

Thematic index

List of judgments and decisions cited (by alphabetical order)

European Court of Human Rights

Abdulaziz, Cabales and Balkandali v. the United Kingdom, 28 May 1985

Buscarini and others v. San Marino [GC], 18 February 1999

Campbell and Cosans v. the United Kingdom, 25 February 1982

Canea Catholic Church v. Greece, 16 December 1997

Case of 97 Members of the Gldani Congregation of Jehovah's Witnesses and Others v. Georgia, 3 May 2007

Case of Freedom and Democracy Party (OZDEP) and others v. Turkey [GC], 8 December 1999

Casimiro v. Luxembourg (dec.), 27 April 1999

Cha'are Shalom Ve Tsedek v. France [GC], 27 June 2000

Church of Scientology Moscow v. Russia, 5 April 2007

Costello-Roberts v. the United Kingdom, 25 March 1993

Dahlab v. Switzerland (dec.), 15 February 2001

Dudgeon v. the United Kingdom, 22 October 1981

Engel and Others v. the Netherlands, 8 June 1976

Folgerø and Others v. Norway [GC], 29 June 2007

Handyside v. the United Kingdom, 7 December 1976

Hasan and Chaush v. Bulgaria [GC], 26 October 2000

Hasan and Eylem Zengin v. Turkey, 9 October 2007

Ilascu and others v. Moldova and Russia [GC], 8 July 2004

Ivanova v. Bulgaria, 12 April 2007

Kalaç v. Turkey , 1 July 1997

Kjeldsen, Busk Madsen and Pederson v. Denmark, 7 December 1976

Kokkinakis v. Greece, 25 May 1993

Köse and Others v. Turkey (dec.), 24 January 2006

Kosteski v. the former Yugoslav Republic of Macedonia, 13 April 2006

Kurtulmus v. Turkey (dec.), 24 January 2006

Kuznetsov v. Russia, 11 January 2007

Larissis and others v. Greece, 24 February 1998

Laskey, Jaggard and Brown v. the United Kingdom, 19 February 1997

Leyla Şahin v. Turkey [GC], 10 November 2005

Manoussakis and Others v. Greece, 26 September 1996

Metropolitan Church of Bessarabia and Others v. Moldova, 13 December 2001

Moscow Branch of the Salvation Army v. Russia, 05 October 2006

Murphy v. Ireland, 10 July 2003

Norwood v. the United Kingdom (dec.), 16 November 2004

Otto-Preminger-Institut v. Austria, 20 September 1994

Pichon and Sajous v. France (dec.), 2 October 2001

Phull v. France (dec.), 11 January 2005

Plattform "Ärzte für das Leben" v. Austria, 21 June 1988

Pretty v. the United Kingdom, 29 April 2002

Refah Partisi (the Welfare Party) and Others v. Turkey, 31 July 2001.

Selmouni v. France [GC], 28 July 1999

Serif v. Greece, 14 December 1999

Socialist Party of Turkey (STP) and Others v. Turkey, 12 November 2003

Sofianopoulos and Others v. Greece (dec.), 12 December 2002

Sunday Times v. the United Kingdom (no. 1), judgment of 26 April 1979

Supreme Holy Council of the Muslim Community v. Bulgaria, 16 December 2004

Thlimmenos v. Greece [GC], 6 April 2000

Valsamis v. Greece, 18 December 1996

Van der Mussele v. Belgium, 23 November 1983

Vogt v. Germany, 26 September 1995

Wingrove v. the United Kingdom, 25 November 1995

Yazar and others v. Turkey, 09 April 2002

European Commission of Human Rights

Arrowsmith v. UK, 12 October 1978

Choudhury v. the United Kingdom, 5 March 1991

Knudsen v. Norway, 8 March 1985

Konttinen v. Finland, 3 December 1996

Stedman v. the United Kingdom, 9 April 1997

X and the Church of Scientology v. Sweden, 5 May 1979

X v. Austria, 1965

X v. the United Kingdom, 12 March 1981

X v. the United Kingdom, 6 March 1982

Other bodies and courts

Boodoo v. Trinidad and Tobago, 2002 (Human Rights Committee of the United Nations)

K. Singh Bhinder v. Canada, 1989 (Human Rights Committee of the Office of the United Nations)

Playfoot v. *Governing Body of Millais School,* 2007 (England and Wales High Court)

R (ex parte Begum) v. Denbigh High School, 2006 (United Kingdom House of Lords)

Riley v. Canada, 2002 (Human Rights Committee of the United Nations)

Glossary

Any person, non-governmental organisation or group of persons that brings a case before the European Court of Human Rights. The right to do so is guaranteed by Article 34 of the European Convention on Human Rights. It is subject to the conditions set out in Article 35 of the Convention.

Applicant

The full title is the "Convention for the Protection of Human Rights and Fundamental Freedoms", usually referred to as "the ECHR" or "the Convention". It was adopted in 1950 and entered into force in 1953. The full text of the Convention and its additional Protocols is available in 30 languages at http://www.echr.coe.int/. The chart of signatures and ratifications as well as the text of declarations and reservations made by State Parties can be consulted at http://conventions.coe.int.

European Convention on Human Rights

The European Court of Human Rights was set up in Strasbourg by the Council of Europe Member States in 1959 to deal with alleged violations of the 1950 European Convention on Human Rights. Since 1 November 1998 it has sat as a full-time Court composed of an equal number of judges to that of the States party to the Convention. The Court examines the admissibility and merits of applications submitted to it. It sits in Chambers of 7 judges or, in exceptional cases, as a Grand Chamber of 17 judges. The Committee of Ministers of the Council of Europe supervises the execution of the Court's judgments.

European Court of Human Rights

The ECHR provides for the limitation of certain rights for the sake of the greater public interest. The European Court of Human Rights has held that when rights are restricted there must be a fair balance between the public interest at stake and the human right in question. The Court is the final arbiter on when this balance has been found. It does however give States a 'margin of appreciation' in assess-

Fair balance

ing whether the public interest is strong enough to justify restrictions on certain human rights. See also margin of appreciation; public interest.

Interference

Any instance where the enjoyment of a right set out in the Convention is limited. Not every interference will mean that there has been a violation of the right in question. Many interferences may be justified by the restrictions provided for in the Convention itself. Generally for an interference to be justified it must be in accordance with the law, pursue a legitimate aim and be proportionate to that aim. See also legitimate aim; prescribed by law; proportionality.

Legitimate aim

This expression is used by the Court in connection with a number of Articles of the Convention: Article 8 (right to respect for private and family life and for home), Article 9 (freedom of thought, conscience and religion), Article 10 (freedom of expression), Article 11 (freedom of assembly and association). While the Convention seeks to safeguard the freedom to manifest one's religion or beliefs, The Court does recognise that, in certain specific circumstances, restrictions may be acceptable. However, the measures imposing such restrictions should meet a number of requirements for the Court not to find a violation of the right in question. One of them is that they should be necessary in a democratic society, which means that they should answer a pressing social need and pursue a legitimate aim. Article 9 lists the broad categories of aims which can be considered as legitimate to justify an interference with the right to freedom of thought, conscience and religion: public safety, public order, health or morals, the protection of the rights and freedoms of others.

Margin of appreciation

The protection offered by the Convention with regard to certain rights is not absolute and provides for the possibility for States to restrict these rights to a certain extent. This is true in the case of the rights covered by Article 9 of the Convention. However, the measures which are taken by the authorities to restrict these rights should meet certain requirements: they should be prescribed by law, necessary in a democratic society and thus pursue a legitimate aim (such as the protection of health or the economic well-being of the country), they should also be proportionate to the aim pursued. Once it establishes that these measures are prescribed by law and are necessary in a democratic society in pursuing a legitimate aim, it has to be examined whether the measures in question are proportionate to this legitimate aim. For this purpose, the Court weighs the interests of the individual against those of the community to decide which prevail in particular circumstances and to what extent the rights encompassed in the Convention could be curtailed in the interests of the community. It is in the context of this examination that the idea that the authorities enjoy a certain "margin of appreciation" has been developed. Indeed, the Court has established that authorities are given a certain scope for discretion, i.e. the "margin of appreciation", in determining the most appropriate measures to take in order to reach the legitimate aim sought. The reason why the Court decided that such leeway should be left to the authorities is that national authorities are often better placed to assess matters falling under the Articles concerned. The scope of this margin of appreciation varies, which means that authorities often have a certain scope for discretion in their actions. However, in no way should this margin of appreciation be seen as absolute and preventing the Court from any critical assessment of the proportionality of the measures concerned.

Positive obligations

The Court's case-law in respect of a number of provisions of the Convention states that public authorities should not only refrain from interfering arbitrarily with individuals' rights as protected expressly by the Articles of the Convention, they should also take active steps to safeguard them. These additional obligations are usually referred to as positive obligations as the authorities are required to act so as to prevent violations of the rights encompassed in the Convention or punish those responsible.

Prescribed by law (in accordance with the law)

The term used in Article 8 paragraph 2 of the Convention is "in accordance with the law" but this is taken to mean the same as the term "prescribed by law" which is found in paragraphs 2 of Articles 9, 10 and 11. The purpose of the term is to ensure that when rights are restricted by public authorities, this restriction is not arbitrary and has some basis in domestic law. The Court has stated for a restriction to meet the requirement it should be adequately accessible and its effects should be foreseeable.

Proportionate measures

By proportionate measures the Court means measures taken by authorities that strike a fair balance between the interests of the community and the interests of an individual.

Religious symbols   Refer to Section VI (b)-(d) of the manual for this notion as
                               well as the wearing of religion symbols in public areas.

Subsidiarity (principle   The principle of subsidiarity is one of the founding prin-
of)   ciples of the human rights protection mechanism of the
                               Convention. According to this principle it should first and
                               foremost be for national authorities to ensure that the
                               rights enshrined in the Convention are not violated and to
                               offer redress if ever they are. The Convention mechanism
                               and the European Court of Human Rights should only be a
                               last resort in cases where the protection or redress needed
                               has not been offered at national level.